A LETTER FROM PETER MUNK

Since we started the Munk Debates, my wife, Melanie, and I have been deeply gratified at how quickly they have captured the public's imagination. From the time of our first event in May 2008, we have hosted what I believe are some of the most exciting public policy debates in Canada and internationally. Global in focus, the Munk Debates have tackled a range of issues, such as humanitarian intervention, the effectiveness of foreign aid, the threat of global warming, religion's impact on geopolitics, the rise of China, and the decline of Europe. These compelling topics have served as intellectual and ethical grist for some of the world's most important thinkers and doers, from Henry Kissinger to Tony Blair, Christopher Hitchens to Paul Krugman, Peter Mandelson to Fareed Zakaria.

The issues raised at the Munk Debates have not only fostered public awareness, but they have also helped many of us become more involved and, therefore, less intimidated by the concept of globalization. It is so easy to be inward-looking. It is so easy to be xenophobic. It is so easy to be nationalistic. It is hard to go into the unknown. Globalization, for many people, is an abstract concept at best. The purpose of this debate series is to help people feel more familiar with our fast-changing world and more comfortable participating in the universal dialogue about the issues and events that will shape our collective future.

I don't need to tell you that that there are many, many burning issues. Global warming, the plight of extreme poverty, genocide, our shaky financial order: these are just a few of the critical issues that matter to people. And it seems to me, and to my foundation board members, that the quality of the public dialogue on these critical issues diminishes in direct proportion to the salience and number of these issues clamouring for our attention. By trying to highlight the most important issues at crucial moments in the global conversation, these debates not only profile the ideas and opinions of some of the world's brightest thinkers, but they also crystallize public passion and knowledge, helping to tackle some of the challenges confronting humankind.

I have learned in life—and I'm sure many of you will share this view—that challenges bring out the best in us. I hope you'll agree that the participants in these debates challenge not only each other but also each of us to think clearly and logically about important problems facing our world.

Peter Munk (1927–2018)
Founder, Aurea Foundation
Toronto, Ontario

POLITICAL CORRECTNESS

DYSON AND GOLDBERG VS. FRY AND PETERSON

THE MUNK DEBATES

Edited by Rudyard Griffiths

ANANSI

Published in Canada in 2018 by House of Anansi Press Inc.
www.houseofanansi.com

22 21 20 19 18   1 2 3 4 5

Library and Archives Canada Cataloguing in Publication

Political correctness : the Munk debates / Michael Eric Dyson, Michelle Goldberg, Stephen Fry, Jordan Peterson.

(The Munk debates)
Issued in print and electronic formats.
ISBN 978-1-4870-0525-2 (softcover).—ISBN 978-1-4870-0526-9 (EPUB).—ISBN 978-1-4870-0527-6 (Kindle)

1. Political correctness. 2. Freedom of speech. 3. Ideology. 4. Social history—21st century. I. Dyson, Michael Eric, panelist II. Goldberg, Michelle, 1975-, panelist III. Fry, Stephen, 1957-, panelist IV. Peterson, Jordan B., panelist V. Series: Munk debates

HM1216.M86 2018   323.44   C2018-904408-X
C2018-904409-8

Cover design: Alysia Shewchuk
Text design and typesetting: Sara Loos
Transcription: Transcript Heroes

Library of Congress Control Number: 2018952735

 Canada Council for the Arts   **Conseil des Arts du Canada**   ONTARIO ARTS COUNCIL
CONSEIL DES ARTS DE L'ONTARIO
an Ontario government agency
un organisme du gouvernement de l'Ontario

We acknowledge for their financial support of our publishing program the Canada Council for the Arts, the Ontario Arts Council, and the Government of Canada.

Printed and bound in Canada

RECYCLED
Paper made from
recycled material
FSC® C103567

CONTENTS

Pre-Debate Interviews with Moderator Rudyard Griffiths

MICHAEL ERIC DYSON IN CONVERSATION WITH RUDYARD GRIFFITHS

RUDYARD GRIFFITHS: It's our pleasure to speak with celebrated author Michael Eric Dyson. He's got a couple of bestselling books under his belt, he teaches at Georgetown University in Washington, D.C., and he's a broadcaster on NPR, ESPN, and elsewhere. Michael, great to have you here in Toronto.

MICHAEL ERIC DYSON: Thanks for having me.

RUDYARD GRIFFITHS: This is the big cultural debate of the moment. I'm sure you don't subscribe to the entire canon of so-called political correctness, but what elements do you think are indicative of progress in our society?

MICHAEL ERIC DYSON: Look, I think people tend to forget that the Left invented political correctness. Not its idea, but the notion that we should be careful and cautious, and not be so sensitive and hypersensitive and exaggerate or excuse certain things that we're doing. So, the Left came up with the concept, but it got hijacked by the Right, and now it seems to mean that everything I'm mad at but can't be bigoted about anymore is politically incorrect. I can't call you names, I can't talk to women the same way, I can't look at Jews or Muslims, and so on.

So, everything is so hush-hush and it's so "politically correct." Well, you want to be correct about a lot of things. If your cheque comes home mathematically incorrect, you're going to be upset. So, yeah, we want correctness in a lot of stuff. Now, there's no exact metric when it comes to politics, but I would say that I'm from a people who have often argued against the mainstream, who've been outside of the parameters of protection of the mainstream. To us, political correctness sounds like people wanting to hold onto the same kind of useless bigotries that used to inform what we did as a nation.

The helpful part is to be self-critical, to take inventory, to examine one's own life, and to figure out ways in which we have indeed lost a sense of challenge. You know, I teach in the university, so I'm critical of some of the moments where people are so sensitive that we can't deal with tough stuff.

Say we're going to talk about something real, like police violence. I'll give a trigger warning: "Here it is. It's coming. Let's grapple with it." I don't dismiss young people's needs for safe space and trigger warnings, but I think the classroom is a robust centre of learning, and sometimes we have to confront ideas we don't like. I believe in more speech, not less. I believe people must counter speech with speech.

Now, that doesn't mean that some speech is not connected to hateful practices and by itself conjures those heinous and hateful practices, but for the most part I think confronting tough issues helps us make advances, and we can say, "Well, that's some good stuff and we can build around it."

RUDYARD GRIFFITHS: I think one argument you're probably going to hear tonight from your opponents is a rebuttal of this idea of privilege, privilege on the part of people who look like your opponents, who are white, or generally further up the class ladder rather than further down, and who are men. And who resent this idea that somehow their voice needs to be understood through the context of their lived historical experience versus, let's say, your community's lived historical experience. How do you respond to people's tension and anxiety and anger about that?

MICHAEL ERIC DYSON: Wow! Really surprising, huh, that people who have benefited from privilege are now mad that it gets called out. Really? You know what amazes me? White men, in particular, who call college students snowflakes. Who's the biggest snowflakin' white man? I'm just trying to figure it out—like, where? "No, Mommy, they won't let us have our toys in the sandbox and we have to share now. But they're mine."

Are you kidding? You're white, male, able-bodied, heterosexual, yeah. I'm a Black man. Am I benefiting from my male status? Of course, because I'm living in a predominantly male society, or at least a patriarchal one. Not numerically but in terms of outlook and ideology and philosophy.

So when I hear white men snowflaking and bitching and kvetching and complaining about privilege—I'm going to talk about it tonight, but I'll just quote that great influence, Keyser Söze, who reputedly said that the greatest thing the devil did is to make people believe he didn't exist. *That's* white male privilege. The greatest thing they can do is try to hide it: "Well? What, what? What do we have?"

I'll tell you what they have: they run most banks, most countries, most universities; they have extraordinary benefits. But people misunderstand: to have white male privilege doesn't mean every white male is privileged. It means you've got a step up, a leg up. In the U.S., we had apartheid, better known as Jim Crow. There was a "white" water fountain and a "black" water fountain, and white folk had most of the resources, but it didn't mean that every white person had the resources. No, it meant that if you were white you had a better chance at success.

But in some ways, this leg up can make things tough. "You mean you're white and you *still* failed? What's up with you?" You started out with an advantage. Well, economic inequality is real, and an economic downturn that affects everybody is real. So we have empathy for white people who struggle against the odds. But at the same time, imagine the odds if your people couldn't even get into the game? Babe Ruth didn't hit seven hundred and some homeruns against the best ball players. He hit them against the best *white* ball players.

And now we see that these Latino and African-American boys are just as good as these white boys, and are giving them a run for their money. When there's a level playing field and the rules are clear, as Jesse Jackson says, white folk have to face up to a fact: "Oh, we've had it best and greatest all along. We controlled the competition. We didn't even let black people into school, into Harvard and Yale and Princeton." Right?

So white men, what speakest thou? How do you conjure this now? Is there going to be resentment? Of course, but is that resentment an index of legitimate and valid complaint? No. You're bitching. Anybody who's had an advantage and who has to give it up is going to be mad, you know? As the great rappers say, "Tell 'em why you're mad, son."

So, no disrespect to my *confrères*, but the reality is that the jig is up. You've had access to Western history for about three, four hundred years, used the Enlightenment to justify your irrational assault upon people's lives. You had enslavement, you had Jim Crow. What, what?! What you complaining about, right? Now we have to share.

You know the guy who killed people here in Toronto — ran them down on Yonge Street — because he couldn't get a date? Get in the game! Learn how to talk to a woman. Do what the rest of us have to do. Let me figure this out. I go to the dance; you turn me down. I get back out there and try again. That's how most of us end up getting married. That's the nature of the game.

But as a white man you feel you have some extra oomph, you have some extra reason and rationale to actually have access to Raquel Welch. No, bro, most people don't, all right? So I think that argument is rather thin and vacuous.

RUDYARD GRIFFITHS: Another argument you're going to hear tonight is the idea that by putting issues of race and gender at the centre of the political conversation, and asserting that people's identities emerge through their gender and their race, you are sowing a tribalism in our society that makes it next to impossible for us to come together around common goals, to pursue common purposes.

MICHAEL ERIC DYSON: Well, we just want to be like white people. I'm sorry, we want to be like y'all! Who started this? I don't think Native Americans started it, I don't think Indigenous people here started it. I'm not sure, but when I check history, it seems that white people invented race. And now that it's out of control, and you've lost the narrative... now you're upset?

Black people did not invent race. People of colour did not invent race. Women didn't invent gender. These are man-made lakes that suck and drown our humanity. So why are we putting race in the middle? Because we have to. "Oh, I'm so sorry, but I'm putting race at the centre of the conversation because police keep killing me in the streets." Or, "At Starbucks you keep calling the police."

Or "If I'm having a barbecue, you call…" Who's putting race in the middle? I'm just trying to have a barbecue!

Or, "I'm a twelve-year-old kid in Cleveland and I'm trying to play with a toy gun and you roll up and in two seconds you kill me." Who's putting race in the middle of that conversation? Now, what our friends on the Right want us to do is to pretend these practices and behaviours don't exist, to live in what Gore Vidal called the United States of Amnesia— or maybe the United Kingdom of Amnesia, or in the United Canadian Amnesia.

But we can't pretend these things don't exist. We can't just wish them away: "Let's not talk about race and class and gender because you're disuniting us." Oh? White was a default position. It didn't have to come out of the closet. It didn't have to announce itself as white. When you're dominant you don't have to announce it. Everything is. When you're doing it, it just is what it is. As the great philosopher Beyoncé Giselle Knowles said when she was handing out an award to Colin Kaepernick, "It's been said that racism is so American that when you challenge racism, it looks like you're challenging America."

There's been an identification of America with certain practices, groups, tribal identities. What's more tribal than a culture that has made a cult out of its own mythic individualism, its massive manhood and masculinity? And when that manhood has been proven to be toxic or deficient or incapable of generating sufficient ideas to sustain us as a nation? Well, it's a spent idea. Then the blame game begins, and then the very people who invented the game get mad that the game is out of hand.

But *you* invented the game. You invented Monopoly and now you're mad you don't have any money left in the game. Learn that these are the rules. You generated them. Hopefully, however, when we talk about race or class or gender or sexual orientation or otherness, we're trying to foreground the humanity of other people.

And so I think it's extremely important to acknowledge that race is what white people invented. David Hume, Immanuel Kant, some of the greatest philosophical minds, deployed their philosophical acuity in defence of their tribal identities. And we have Thomas Jefferson, writing notes in Virginia during the day questioning the rational capacity of the Negro, but at night he's linking with Sally Hemings. His loins trumped his logic. Thank God.

The reality is that when we look at the history of the development and evolution of the idea of whiteness and of a Canadian or American or European identity, white folk have got a lot of skin in the game. They literally invented this thing, and now that it's beyond their control and they aren't exactly benefiting from it, they complain — or they exaggerate their victimhood.

Again, going back to white men who complain about people being snowflakes, I have never seen such a culture of complaint, a culture of whining. They could have their own vineyards. It's just whine, whine, whine, whine, whine! "Burgundy and blush," and, you know … "Zinfandel"! Just emotional whining that is astonishing! And I think we've just got to call it for what it is.

RUDYARD GRIFFITHS: Well, you've called it for what it is.

MICHAEL ERIC DYSON: Thanks, Rudyard.

RUDYARD GRIFFITHS: Michael, thanks for coming to Toronto. I'm going to enjoy so much moderating you onstage this evening.

MICHAEL ERIC DYSON: I'm looking forward to it, my brother.

MICHELLE GOLDBERG IN CONVERSATION WITH RUDYARD GRIFFITHS

RUDYARD GRIFFITHS: I'm here with Michelle Goldberg, columnist at the *New York Times*, award-winning author, and television commentator on MSNBC and elsewhere. She's going to be speaking for the motion tonight. It's terrific to have you in Toronto, Michelle.

MICHELLE GOLDBERG: Thanks for having me.

RUDYARD GRIFFITHS: So, give us your opening gambit here.

MICHELLE GOLDBERG: Okay — and I'm going to say this onstage — when you first presented me with this motion, I balked a bit, because there are a lot of things that fall under the rubric of political correctness that I don't consider progress. And I've been really critical in my columns of "no-platforming," of some of the excesses of social justice culture on college campuses.

But one thing that made it a little bit easier to speak in support of this resolution was the people that I'm debating, because certainly what Jordan Peterson calls political correctness, I call progress. He describes almost any efforts to rectify or acknowledge discrimination against women or sexual or gender minorities as a politically correct assault on the natural order.

I think this is less so the case with Stephen Fry. There's probably more overlap between my thinking and his, although I would disagree, for example, with his fierce opposition to tearing down statues of figures that we now revile, just because I think cultures change and people should be allowed to decide who they honour and celebrate and commemorate.

RUDYARD GRIFFITHS: You're going to hear an argument tonight, probably from both Fry and Peterson, about this idea that at the core of the Enlightenment, at the core of the Western project, is a belief in the assertion of the individual and individuals' ability to define themselves, to speak their minds, and to do this regardless of the harm it might create for marginalized groups. Where do you come down on that debate?

MICHELLE GOLDBERG: One of the things that's going to be interesting is that we have debaters from three different countries, with three very different understandings of free speech and hate speech laws. I have, I think, an American liberal free speech conception, and there are hate speech laws here in Canada and in the U.K. that would never fly in America and that are very foreign to me.

I'm not a big supporter of hate speech laws. I'm somewhat of a civil libertarian on the topic. I think this dichotomy between the assertion of the individual and the rights of the group is kind of a false dichotomy. When you have discrimination against groups, it impedes the ability of individuals to fully express themselves and realize their potential.

There would be no rights for individual women or individual people of colour without the movements on behalf of groups that allowed the individuals in those groups to realize themselves. And so, again, I would reject the idea that there is a contradiction between individual freedom and movements on behalf of civil rights for groups of people. And I would also say that I actually think *our* side is the side of the Enlightenment, the side of saying that...

RUDYARD GRIFFITHS: Are we talking about the idea of dignity here, and the promulgation of diversity?

MICHELLE GOLDBERG: The idea of being able to change culture, of not being beholden to traditional structures of the ever-expanding circle of human freedom; that's an Enlightenment idea. The idea that the social order is extremely fragile and must be protected at all costs or at almost all costs, which is an idea that courses through Mr. Peterson's work, is to me much more at odds with the Enlightenment.

RUDYARD GRIFFITHS: You've written a lot on identity politics. What's your view of the criticism of identity politics that states that by putting race and issues of gender and class at the very centre of our discourse, we are denuding ourselves of the capacity to find common ground, to develop a shared consensus, to pursue common goals? This is all very tribal, and—in the views of Jordan Peterson and maybe Stephen Fry—very destructive.

MICHELLE GOLDBERG: It's interesting that you put it like that, because the way it usually plays out in the United States is that centring on issues of gender and race and maybe sexual identity stands in contrast to a class-based politics, right? I mean, there is no politics that doesn't have opposing groups or opposing interests. That's what politics is—the contention of opposing groups. It's a question of which groups.

The criticism in the United States has been that identity politics, race, and gender often come at the expense of class and have ended up undermining the New Deal coalition. But, at least as far as the United States goes, the problem is that the New Deal coalition foundered on the shoals of race. It fell apart in response to the civil rights movement, and so you can't go around that. You have to go through it, you have to deal with it head on unless you're willing to constantly say that the rights of women and racial minorities are going to be subordinate.

RUDYARD GRIFFITHS: Another argument you'll hear tonight from your opponents is about men and women, and about the conversation we're currently having around the #MeToo movement. I would expect we're going to hear a case that we're in a cultural panic about the power of men and the supposed subjection of women. What's your view on that, and how do you think it's going to play out?

MICHELLE GOLDBERG: You know, it's interesting. The #MeToo movement just started in what, September? And within three months—not even—just a few weeks, suddenly everybody was saying, "Oh my God! Have we gone too far?" But when you actually look at who has been taken down, the idea that it's become this all-encompassing Stalinist inquisition is a bit of an exaggeration. I mean, to go to prison, Bill Cosby had to have two trials and any number of women telling similar stories of the most brutal sorts of rape.

And Harvey Weinstein—yes, he lost his career, but only after being accused credibly and repeatedly with hard evidence of payouts by many, many women. And the people who have lost their positions and lost their jobs—not lost their lives, not lost their freedoms, lost their jobs—it hasn't been just because of a McCarthyist rumour; it's been because there have been multiple, independently corroborated stories with hard evidence.

And yet, it's so unusual that any men at all are losing their jobs. Or that anybody is suffering consequences. It really is something new, and I think that's where the cultural panic comes from; it's panic about the end of male impunity.

RUDYARD GRIFFITHS: Do you think men need to think about the historical privileges that have been conferred on them and maybe, if not step aside then at least make some more space for women, and for other groups who've been historically disadvantaged?

MICHELLE GOLDBERG: I actually think that the things we're asking of men maybe start a little smaller than that. Like, never take out your penis at work.

You know, honestly, I feel like women are not asking. They're saying, "Yeah, maybe think about if you have a panel and it's all men, and particularly if you're discussing women's issues, maybe don't do that," you know? I feel like there's such a huge gap between what is being asked of men and what some men perceive to be being asked of them.

And that is part of the debate tonight, right? I think that the men I know, the men I work with, are sort of conscious of trying to promote more women and, for example, to make sure that women and men are paid equally when they're doing equal work, when they're at the same stature in a company. But I don't think we're asking for men to go through some kind of Stalinist re-education camps.

RUDYARD GRIFFITHS: Final question, Michelle. Do you think this debate boils down in some ways to a conversation about civility? I mean, if you look at so-called political correctness, and people using that word pejoratively, is a lot of what they're criticizing simply about attitudes, inclinations on behalf of groups and individuals and institutions to try to behave toward one another with a greater sense of civility?

MICHELLE GOLDBERG: Yes, I think that some of what they're asking for is maybe better manners. It's interesting to look back on the last panic about political correctness in the late '80s and early '90s. Back then, what people really found unbearable about political correctness was that suddenly you couldn't refer to Indigenous people as Indians anymore, and you couldn't use "retard" as a pejorative. And you weren't supposed to refer to the adult women you worked with as girls. And that really stuck in people's throats, right? You couldn't make gay jokes!

Most of those things have now been seamlessly integrated to the point where we wouldn't even think to use that kind of language—I mean, presumably. It doesn't really feel oppressive that we can't use that language; it just feels like that language seems unkind and sort of retrograde.

I think something similar is happening here. Some of these changes initially feel unnatural to people; they kind of stick in their throats. The ones that work and have social utility will seamlessly become integrated into the language, and the ones that don't will fall away, just as some of the more outré demands of previous periods of political ferment have fallen away.

RUDYARD GRIFFITHS: Michelle, thank you so much. Great to have you here in Toronto. We look forward to your appearance on the Munk Debate stage tonight.

MICHELLE GOLDBERG: Thank you so much.

STEPHEN FRY IN CONVERSATION WITH
RUDYARD GRIFFITHS

RUDYARD GRIFFITHS: We're now speaking with Stephen Fry: actor, comedian, Emmy Award winner — the list goes on and on — poet, and tonight a debater. Stephen, it's great to have you here at the Munk Debates.

STEPHEN FRY: Thank you, Rudyard. A pleasure.

RUDYARD GRIFFITHS: Why is an avowed champion of LGBT rights taking part in this debate and arguing on the same side as Jordan Peterson?

STEPHEN FRY: I came because I think it's very important to try to suggest that any anti-PC rhetoric isn't entirely the property of the Right. I characterize myself as a soft leftie — a flaccid, flabby leftie — not a progressive or a street-marching socialist but someone who's always tended toward a liberal outlook.

And I'm aware of how under threat that outlook is and also how it is regarded by the new Right as being in charge. We who were once the outsiders knocking in and being subversive and transgressive and saying naughty things, and refusing to toe the line of authority, are now under threat, particularly in academia, which seems to be the battleground now. That is not where I work, but I'm familiar with it and have spent quite a lot of time there, and I have a lot of friends in academia. Where once it was a battleground that the Left were trying to infiltrate, it's now one that the Right are trying to infiltrate.

For the same reasons that the Left were allowed to make their fuss and to shout and demonstrate and so on in the days of the '60s — you know, post-'68 — so it is important that the Right is able to do so today. After all, if people are going to say that the purpose of political correctness is to celebrate diversity, then that diversity must include diversity of opinion. If it doesn't, it's meaningless.

RUDYARD GRIFFITHS: What other elements of the so-called politically correct movement do you think are undermining our sense of shared efficacy, a culture that we celebrate in terms of its openness?

STEPHEN FRY: Actually, the free speech side of it is important, but it's not what I would emphasize. For all the things I hate about PC, stylistically and just viscerally — sanctimony, piety, self-righteousness, resentment and anger, orthodoxy, accusation, denunciation, shaming... All of these are vile, and I'm not saying I'd put up with them, but they're not as important as the fact that it simply doesn't work. That's what I would emphasize. It does the *opposite* of work. It's a recruiting sergeant for the Right.

All it takes is a bit of imagination to think of a white young man of eighteen going to university. Say he's confused and not necessarily "woke" in the political sense. What's he going to think of all this stridency and these shouts of "white privilege" here and "heteronormative" there, and just all of this jargonistic claptrap? It's so stupid. I think that's the point; it's just dumb.

In chess, which I used to be a lover of, there was an old saying. I think it was Max Euwe, one of the Dutch players, who said, "The best move in chess is not the best chess move; it's the move your opponent least wants you to play. That's the best move." And that goes all the way back to *The Art of War*, you know. You must put yourself in the place of the person you want to persuade or to defeat.

And I don't think PC does that. I think PC, as I say, is just a recruiting sergeant. I think if I were seventeen or eighteen now and going to university, it would make me think, "Sod that!" I mean, I'm a natural contrarian like Christopher Hitchens, a natural transgressive. I want to shake things up, I want to disagree with what I consider orthodoxy — I'm heterodox — almost as a matter of pride. You just don't go with the flow, you try to stand alone.

And so I think for the Left, if it wants to achieve all the things that it should, it's a question of how you achieve the golden aim of making a more tolerant society, not simply prescribing language and forcing people to use uncomfortable and silly phrases. And I hope I don't have to repeat that I'm against homophobia, transphobia, Islamophobia, xenophobia, all the phobias...against bigotry, racism, intolerance of all kinds.

One of the huge errors people make on the Left is to underestimate the smartness of the enemy, as it were. It may be that the Trumps of this world don't read the same sacred liberal arts texts that we regard as the important building blocks of an intelligence, but it doesn't mean they're not cunning and smart. It really doesn't. It's so stupid to underestimate them, as history shows—really dumb.

RUDYARD GRIFFITHS: One of the arguments you will no doubt hear tonight is that there are different social goals. Freedom of speech—the assertion of individual choice—may be one, but people also say we're living in very diverse, complex societies. Inclusion should trump some of the...

STEPHEN FRY: Yeah, I know. It's unfortunate that you can't use the word "trump" anymore. We'll have to find a new verb.

RUDYARD GRIFFITHS: Some say inclusion should be the primary goal for institutions, maybe even for societies, because by bringing people together through a respect for diversity and difference, we're building healthier, stronger societies. You know the line.

STEPHEN FRY: I know the line, and of course it's right. But if you think the way to do it is to force people to use a language and to recognize a kind of preposterous post-structuralist hermeneutics on the one side, or just a flabby hopefulness on the other...I don't think it's right.

You know, let's just look at human wit and see. I taught at a school before I went to university—just this little job while I was in my gap year—and it was around the time it was decided that the word "handicapped" would not be used, but "challenged" would. And this was in the papers; it was an early example of political correctness. I'm talking about 1979 or so.

And I remember these school kids. One of them fell over and the other pointed to him and went, "Challenged!" You just immediately co-opt the word for your own wicked humour, and rightly so; I applaud it, you know. And if someone wants to shout "Faggot!" I don't care as a gay man. I know I'm supposed to, but I'm supposed to care on behalf of people who are supposedly weaker than me, and I think it's the most patronizing thing in the world.

It's exactly the same political correctness I grew up with, which then was a kind of religious political correctness—people complaining about television programs because there was swearing or violence or nudity. They would say, "I'm not shocked myself; it's just the vulnerable young minds, you see." Oh, fuck that! That's just not good enough, it really isn't.

And that's my objection. It's denouncing from the pulpit. Russia has political correctness, only Russia's political correctness is that you can't say Tchaikovsky was gay.

You know, there's a right-wing political correctness. To use the word "redneck" is considered offensive, and so on, so it's not something that actually only belongs to one side. It's a way of shutting down debate. It's a way of formalizing. I mean, you've only got to read *Darkness at Noon* to see this at its most extreme. It always starts off with an ideal and a hopeful goal—equality of societies, how communism began, the French Revolution, equality, fraternity, liberty, all those wonderful things.

The French Revolution ended up with the Committee of General Security, which had a law passed. It said you could take a piece of paper saying something like "Citoyen du Roque is an enemy of the Revolution," put it in the central square on a post, and that person would be arrested. It's basically the same as tweeting it; it's exactly the same idea. It's a denunciation, a shaming without evidence, an assertion.

And all of these things are done for the best possible reasons. As Thomas Cranmer, who wrote the *Book of Common Prayer*—you know, the founder of the Anglican Church, really—said, "There was not anything by the wit of man devised that hath not been in time, in whole or in part, corrupted." It's all very well to say how noble the ideals were, because they're always noble. But you end up with the pigs wearing trousers, to use an Orwellian phrase.

And that's what's happened. Essentially, the left wing won the battle for the campus and it's now middle-aged left-wing baby boomers who are running it. And they're wearing the trousers and insisting what is true and what is not true, and what is acceptable and what is not acceptable. In the name of diversity and inclusion and equality and all the good things, a lot of bad things are being done.

And it's delaying the day when people are more included and more diversities welcomed, I think. That's the problem: it's empowering the enemy.

RUDYARD GRIFFITHS: Final question, Stephen. Where do you think this debate goes from here? Is this a kind of paroxysm that will pass in the same way as the debate in the late '80s and '90s on college campuses?

You could even ask, "Look, are there reverberations to 1968?" Or do you think something much more fundamental is going on, that a new tribalism is emerging in society?

STEPHEN FRY: I don't know. I've given up any confidence in being able to predict the future. I couldn't have predicted three years ago what the world would be like now, right?

And I'm not alone in that. Nobody could and nobody did. And even among people who pretended they did, show me the article in which they wrote what the state of the world would be like now. No one has done it. And the faster and more complex it gets, the more unpredictable it gets — the more chaotic, the more turbulent, the more non-linear the equation is, if you like.

So, it's very difficult to predict. I would only say that there are cycles within the turbulence and so on. I'm a great believer in the Roman idea of the Rota Fortunae, the wheel of fortune. I can remember when Tony Blair in my country, and Clinton in America, and social democrats around Europe were absolutely in power. It was an unquestioned and, it seemed, an inevitable thing that this was the way politics would be — somewhere between sort of centre-left, and sometimes sort of centre-right.

But the wheel went down, and now those people are at the very bottom, and what's at the very top is quite the opposite. But I do believe that means that what's at the top is also on the way down, so I'm not in that sense too pessimistic. And I do believe in humans and humanity.

The best thing that could ever happen for the tribalism and the nationalism, of course, would be an invasion from another planet. It would be the same as when the first astronauts looked back at the Earth and said, "God, the weird thing is you can't see any borders." There's no forty-ninth parallel visible. There's no border between Germany and France or between Russia and China. It's just all one landmass.

Similarly, if the Martians or Venusians come and attack us, suddenly we're not going to worry about, "Oh, but you're a Catholic" or "You're a Jew" or "You're Islamic." I mean, please — that's what we need: a wider cause to belong to.

RUDYARD GRIFFITHS: Stephen, thank you so much for your time today. We look forward to your appearance on the stage tonight.

STEPHEN FRY: Thank you, it's a pleasure.

JORDAN PETERSON IN CONVERSATION WITH RUDYARD GRIFFITHS

RUDYARD GRIFFITHS: Our guest now is Jordan Peterson. He's a professor of psychology at the University of Toronto, a YouTube sensation, and the author of the internationally bestselling book *12 Rules for Life: An Antidote to Chaos.*

RUDYARD GRIFFITHS: Tell us about the last little while for you. You've been on quite a ride.

JORDAN PETERSON: Yes. Since October 2016, I guess, it's been nonstop scandal and entertainment, fundamentally, but for me also a tremendous amount of good. Most of this has been cast in the media, I would say, as a political issue, but it's not a political issue for me. What I've been concentrating on mostly is psychological work at the level of the individual, which is the appropriate level for me, given that I'm a clinical psychologist.

And I'm out on this tour now. I think I've talked in twenty-six cities already and there are, I think, something like sixty more lined up. And it's maybe one person in thirty who I talk to afterwards who has anything political to say; the rest of it is all focused on my lectures, essentially, and the book, and on people's attempts to put their lives together, again at the individual level.

And so that's a really good thing as far as I'm concerned. It's a very rare day now if I go outside that I'll not be approached by four or five people — it doesn't matter where I go — and they all tell me the same thing. They're all very polite and very welcoming. I haven't had a negative interaction with anyone in public at all. Quite the contrary.

They tell me they've been watching my lectures and that they were unhappy in their relationships, or not doing particularly well at their careers, or in a dark place for one reason or another, and that watching and listening to what I've been saying has been very helpful to them. And so, that's great.

RUDYARD GRIFFITHS: How would you say what you've been writing and thinking about, and people's reaction to it, intersects with tonight's debate? Because you've been quite vocal on the topic of political correctness.

JORDAN PETERSON: Well, I'm no fan of the radical Left, so people might say, "Well, does that mean you support the radical Right?" Just because you're no fan of the radical Left doesn't mean you support the radical Right. That's absolutely a preposterous proposition. But the universities, especially the humanities and social sciences, are absolutely dominated by left-wing thinking. That's well documented by people like Jonathan Haidt; it's not my imagination.

And I find the doctrine that unites them to be unconscionably pernicious. It's basically a collectivist doctrine. And here's what disturbs me about it. There's every reason to have a left wing; you need a left wing partly because being left-wing is in part temperamental; it's not going away. And also because, when our society produces hierarchies, which it will inevitably do, people tend to stack up at the bottom. It's in the nature of hierarchies to produce that as an outcome.

And what that means is that the people who are dispossessed in the hierarchical arrangements need a voice, and that's the Left, obviously, and fair enough. But it's also obvious that just as the Right can go too far, the Left can go too far as well. But when the Left goes too far, it's something that's very ill-defined, and to me that's not acceptable. And I think they've certainly gone too far in the universities.

And the postmodern, neo-Marxist pastiche that makes up the radical Left philosophy that's at the bottom of the social sciences and humanities now has nothing about it that's useful, as far as I'm concerned. It has nothing to do with compassion; it has nothing to do with my lack of … what would you say?

RUDYARD GRIFFITHS: Empathy?

JORDAN PETERSON: Precisely. They're completely separate issues. And that's another thing that really bothers me about political correctness. It's like: "Well, we have hammerlock on empathy." First of all, empathy is not enough. It's not even close to enough, and an excess of empathy can do terrible things. And secondly, no you don't have a hammerlock on empathy, and to ally that with a philosophy that essentially assigns people to their identity via their group membership, and then to read not only the current state of affairs but history itself as a battleground between competing groups is, I think, dangerous. I think it's obvious that it's dangerous if you know anything about history.

RUDYARD GRIFFITHS: One argument you're sure to hear tonight is the idea that the privilege people like you and I have enjoyed historically in society by virtue of our race, our class, our gender — that it's time for that privilege to be shared more equitably across groups who've been historically disadvantaged.

JORDAN PETERSON: That's a good example of the conflation of empathy with ideology. First of all, the majority in any society has privilege. That's the whole point of a society: to set up a system so that the bulk of the people in the system can do well, and then you build in protection for minorities. So, to conflate that with race is not acceptable. It's a kind of toxic sleight of hand and it's extraordinarily dangerous.

Apart from that, it's an empty claim. Some people have advantages that other people don't. Well, obviously. And if you take anyone apart into the multitude of categories that they can be taken apart into, what you will find is that on some of those dimensions they're doing better than other people, sometimes for rather arbitrary reasons, and on other dimensions they're doing worse.

The next part of that is: Well, historically speaking, over what span of time do you mean, precisely? Do you mean because my ancestors 150 years ago were privileged, comparatively speaking, that I should somehow pay for that now? And are you so sure my ancestors were privileged? As far as I can tell—take my grandparents on my father's side—my father grew up in a log cabin until he was five; it had three rooms. My grandmother was a cleaning woman for farms in central Saskatchewan in the 1930s. She cooked for threshing crews. She chopped woodpiles that were as big as the damned cabin to get through the winter. So, where's the privilege? I see it accrues to me as a consequence of my race. Oh, I see. So now we're going to have a discussion about race, are we?

And that's the thing about the toxic Left: everything is about group identity. And so, let's take the argument even further and say, okay, well, because of my skin colour I'm differentially privileged, from a historical perspective. So what? You're going to make everybody now pay for some historical inequity on the basis of their race?

And you're going to view the history of the relationships between men and women as one fundamentally of oppression? That's the way we're going to play this, that it wasn't that men and women cooperated throughout history to bring themselves out of the fundamental catastrophe that history has always been? That isn't what it was, despite the fact that in 1895, the typical person in the Western world lived on less than a dollar a day by today's standards, which is far below the UN's current guidelines for abject poverty. We're going to revisit that and we're going to say, "No, really, the fundamental reality of the world was that men oppressed women"?

RUDYARD GRIFFITHS: So that brings me to a second argument you're no doubt going to hear tonight, which is that men need to check their privilege; the idea that among women in particular—the #MeToo movement—there's been an awareness, an awakening about the power of women in society, and that it's time for that to be acknowledged. What will be your response?

JORDAN PETERSON: First of all, when the discussion is about power, it immediately sends a shudder up my spine, partly because part of the postmodern doctrine, especially in its alliance with neo-Marxism—which is the world's strangest alliance, by my estimate—states that everything is about power. And I don't believe that. I think hierarchies are only about power when they've already transformed themselves into tyrannies, and I don't think the fundamental hierarchies that characterize the West are tyrannical, comparatively speaking.

Compared to the heavenly hierarchy in your utopian imagination, no doubt they're exemplars of pure hell, but compared to everywhere else in the world right now and every other hierarchy throughout history, we're doing pretty damned well.

And the fact is that once we had reliable birth control, which really only happened in the 1960s, women were welcomed most fundamentally—although also opposed, but most fundamentally welcomed—into every position of authority and competence that could possibly be laid open to them, to the point where now they make up something damned near three-quarters of humanities and social sciences students. They dominate the health care fields.

So how fast do you expect a transformation to take place? The argument is: well, it would never have happened without political pressure. No...sorry. What triggered it was reliable birth control. And that made it possible. It was reliable birth control, reliable menstrual sanitation, and all of those things that no one ever takes into account that made the playing field open. And it's transformed utterly in, what, fifty years? How fast do you think these things can happen?

RUDYARD GRIFFITHS: Good point.

JORDAN PETERSON: And I'm certainly not against equality of opportunity. What has to be wrong with you to be against equality of opportunity? Even if you're selfish—if you're not absolutely out for destruction and you're *only* selfish, let's say—anybody with any sense would go for equality of opportunity, at least because it gives you the possibility of exploiting the maximal number of qualified and talented people.

And equality of outcome, well...

RUDYARD GRIFFITHS: We'll save that for the debate tonight. Final question I'm asking all of you, pre-debate: Where do you think this debate is going to go from here? Do you think we're in a kind of cultural spasm or do you think there's something more fundamental happening, a new tribalism, a new set of antagonisms that are going to take much longer to work out? What are you seeing?

JORDAN PETERSON: I think it'll depend on how well we each behave in the next ten years, because I think things could get way better everywhere, really fast. Or we could degenerate back into our idiot twentieth-century tribalisms.

I would say there's plenty of pressure in both directions. You know, I'm heartened by the fact that so many people have been taking the psychological material that I've been providing online to heart, and doing what they can to put themselves together.

I'm disheartened by the fact that virtually everything now is transformed into a polarized political argument, and there seems to be no understanding of the fact that not everything is political. I actually don't think the discussion about political correctness is political. I think it's both theological and philosophical, but it's always presented, or often presented, in politicized terms, not least because, if you're influenced by the radical leftist collectivist ideology, that is the *only* playing field. It's all hierarchies at each other's throats playing power games.

The free speech thing is really interesting because on the radical Left, there is no debate about free speech. You can't have a debate about free speech from that ideological position because there isn't any such thing. All there is is those who are manoeuvring for power within their respective groups, making claims that benefit them. That's the basic axiom of the interpretive system.

So, the reason free speech has become politicized is that if you adopt the collectivist viewpoint, it's a shibboleth, it's a fantasy. You might think you're speaking freely but you're not; you're just expressing your privilege.

RUDYARD GRIFFITHS: Speaking on behalf of my gender, my class, my race.

JORDAN PETERSON: Absolutely. And yeah, one of the things about the postmodern insistence on identity that I think is comical in a very, very dark way is the emergence of intersectionality, because the intersectional theorists actually identified the Achilles heel of the collectivist perspective. What they pointed out was: "Well, let's say we cover the standard groups"—I don't know why these are the standard groups, but let's say sex, ethnicity, and race, for the sake of argument—well, what about how they interact? It's like, yeah, what about that? And what about the fact that gender is infinitely differential, not least from the left-wing perspective. And what about the fact that there are endless numbers of ethnic variants. What're you going to do? You're going to control for the interaction between all of those? And the answer is, yes, that's what we'll try to do before we give up our ideology. But the fact of the matter is that the reason the West decided on a radical, individualist perspective to begin with is that we figured out 2,000 years ago, at least at the origins of this type of thinking, that everyone is unique, to the point where you can fractionate their group identity right down to the level of the individual.

I don't know what's going to happen. I think the universities, for example, have done themselves in. I don't think they can escape that. I've watched large organizations crumble, and that can happen very often. One serious error will do it.

RUDYARD GRIFFITHS: Thank you, Jordan. I appreciate your passion and your willingness to step onto the stage and engage with other people's ideas in a spirit of free and open exchange.

JORDAN PETERSON: Well, hopefully it'll go well and it'll be an intelligent discussion and we'll get somewhere.

Political Correctness

Pro: Michael Eric Dyson and Michelle Goldberg
Con: Stephen Fry and Jordan Peterson

May 18, 2018
Toronto, Ontario

RUDYARD GRIFFITHS: Ladies and gentlemen, welcome. My name is Rudyard Griffiths and it's my privilege to moderate tonight's debate.

I want to start by welcoming the North America–wide television audience tuning in right now across Canada on CPAC, Canada's public affairs channel; across the continental United States on C-SPAN; and to those listening on CBC Radio's *Ideas*.

A warm hello also to our online audience watching this debate — the over 6,000 streams active at this very moment — on Facebook Live, Bloomberg.com, and at Munkdebates.com. It's great to have you as virtual participants in tonight's proceedings.

And hello to you, the over 3,000 people who've filled Roy Thomson Hall for yet another Munk Debate. Thank you for your continued support of high-quality debates on the big issues of the day.

This debate marks the start of our tenth season, and we begin it missing someone who was vital to this debate series in every aspect. It was his passion for ideas, his love for debate, that inspired our creation in 2008, and it was his energy, his generosity, and his drive that were so important in allowing us to win international acclaim as one of the world's great debating series.

His philanthropy, his legacy is remarkable. We all remember the $100 million donation to cardiac health here in Toronto last fall, which will transform the lives of millions of Canadians to come. We are all big fans and supporters of the terrific Munk School for Global Affairs and Public Policy on the University of Toronto campus, represented here tonight by many students in its master's program. Congratulations to you. And also, we must recall what a generous endowment he made last spring to this series, one that will allow us to organize many more evenings like this, for many more years to come.

Now, knowing our benefactor as we do, we know that the last thing he'd want is for us to mark his absence with a moment of silence—that wasn't his style. So let's instead celebrate a great Canadian, a great life, and the great legacy of the late Peter Munk. Bravo, Peter!

Thank you, everybody. I know he would have enjoyed that applause. And I want to thank Melanie, Anthony, and Cheyne for being here tonight to be part of Peter's continuing positive impact on public debate in Canada. Thank you for coming.

We have a terrific debate lined up for you this evening. Let's introduce first our "pro" team, arguing *for* tonight's motion, "Be it resolved, what you call political correctness, I call progress." Please welcome to the stage award-winning writer, scholar, and broadcaster on NPR, Michael Eric Dyson.

Michael's debating partner is also an award-winning author. She's a columnist at the *New York Times*, and someone who is going to bring a very distinct and powerful perspective tonight, Michelle Goldberg.

One great team of debaters deserves another. Arguing against our resolution, "Be it resolved, what you call political correctness, I call progress," is the Emmy Award–winning actor, screenwriter, author, playwright, journalist, poet and, tonight, debater, Stephen Fry.

Stephen's teammate is a professor of psychology at the University of Toronto, a YouTube sensation, and the author of the international bestseller *12 Rules for Life*. Ladies and gentlemen, Toronto's Jordan Peterson.

On the way in this evening, we asked this audience of roughly 3,000 to vote on the resolution, "Be it resolved, what you call political correctness, I call progress." Let's see the results. The pre-debate vote: 36 percent agree; 64 percent disagree. So, a room in play.

Now, we also asked how many of you are open to changing your vote over the course of tonight's debate. Are you fixed in your opinion, or could you potentially be convinced by one of these two teams to move your vote over the next hour and a half? Let's see those numbers now: 87 percent said yes; 13 percent said no. So, a very open-minded crowd. This debate is very much in play.

As per the agreed-upon order of speakers, I'm going to call on Michelle Goldberg first for her six minutes of opening remarks.

MICHELLE GOLDBERG: Thank you for having me. As Rudyard knows, I initially balked at the resolution that we're debating tonight, because there are a lot of things that fall under the rubric of political correctness that I *don't* call progress. I don't like "no-platforming" or trigger warnings. Like a lot of middle-aged liberals, I find many aspects of student social justice culture off-putting—although I'm not sure that that particular generation gap is anything new on the record about the toxicity of social media call-out culture, and I think it's good to debate people whose ideas I don't like, which is why I'm here.

So, if there are social justice warriors in the audience, I feel like I should apologize to you, because you're probably going to feel that I'm not adequately defending your ideas. But the reason I'm on this side of the stage is that political correctness isn't just a term for left-wing excesses on college campuses, or people being terrible on Twitter. I think it can be used, especially as deployed by Mr. Peterson, as a way to delegitimize any attempt for women and racial and sexual minorities to overcome discrimination, or even to argue that such discrimination is real.

In the *New York Times* today, Mr. Peterson is quoted as saying: "The people who hold that our culture is an oppressive patriarchy, they don't want to admit that the current hierarchy might be predicated on competence." That's not particularly insane to me, because I'm an American and our president is Donald Trump, but it's an assumption that I think underlies a world view in which any challenges to the current hierarchy are written off as political correctness.

I also think we should be clear that this isn't really a debate about free speech. Mr. Peterson once referred to what he called "the evil trinity of equity, diversity, and inclusivity" and said: "Those three words, if you hear people mouth those three words, equity, diversity and inclusivity, you know who you're dealing with and you should step away from that, because it is not acceptable."

He argues that the movie *Frozen* is politically correct propaganda, and at one point he floated the idea of creating a database of university course content so students could avoid postmodern critical theory.

So, in the criticism of political correctness, I sometimes hear an attempt to purge our thought of certain analytical categories that mirrors, I think, the worst caricatures of the social justice Left that wants to get rid of anything that smacks of colonialism or patriarchy or white supremacy.

I also don't really think we're debating the value of the Enlightenment, at least not in the way that somebody like Mr. Fry, who I think is a champion of Enlightenment values, frames it. The efforts to expand rights and privileges, once granted just to landowning, white, heterosexual men, is the Enlightenment, or it's very much in keeping with the Enlightenment. To quote a dead white man, John Stuart Mill: "The despotism of custom is everywhere the standing hindrance to human advancement."

I think that some of our opponents, by contrast, bring challenges to the despotism of custom as politically correct attacks on a transcendent natural order.

To quote Mr. Peterson again, each gender, each sex, has its own unfairness to deal with, but to think of it as a consequence of the social structure—come on, really, what about nature itself? But there's an exception to this, because he does believe in social interventions to remedy some kinds of unfairness, which is why in the *New York Times*, he calls for "enforced monogamy to remedy the woes of men who don't get their equal distribution of sex."

When it comes to the political correctness debate, we've been here before. Allan Bloom, the author of *The Closing of the American Mind*, compared the "tyranny" of feminism in academia to the Khmer Rouge, and he was writing at a time when women accounted for 10 percent of all college tenured faculty.

It's worth looking back at what was considered annoyingly, outrageously, politically correct in the 1980s, the last time we had this debate. You know, not being able to call Indigenous people "Indians," or having to use hyphenated terms, at least in the United States, terms like African-American. You know, adding women or people of colour to the Western Civilization curriculum, or not making gay jokes or using "retard" as an epithet. I get it: new concepts, new words stick in your throat. The way we're used to talking and thinking seems natural and normal, by definition. And then the new terms, new concepts that have social utility, stick, and those that don't fall away. If you go back to the 1970s, Ms.—you know, *M-S*, as an alternative to Miss or Mrs.—stuck around. And "womyn" with a *y* didn't. And I hope that someday we'll look back and marvel at the idea that gender-neutral pronouns ever seemed like an existential threat to anyone.

But I also don't think it's clear. That might not happen because, if you look around the world right now, there are plenty of places that have indeed dialed back cosmopolitanism and reinstated patriarchy in the name of staving off chaos. And they seem like terrible places to live.

I come from the United States, which is currently undergoing a monumental attempt to roll back social progress in the name of overcoming political correctness. And as someone who lives there, I assure you, it feels nothing like progress. Thank you.

RUDYARD GRIFFITHS: Great start to the debate, Michelle. Thank you. I'm now going to ask Jordan Peterson to speak for the "con" team.

JORDAN PETERSON: Hello. So, we should first decide what we're talking about. We're *not* talking about my views on political correctness, despite what you might have inferred from the last speaker's comments.

This is how it looks to me: we essentially need something approximating a low-resolution grand narrative to unite us. And we need a narrative to unite us because otherwise we don't have peace.

What's playing out in the universities and in broader society right now is a debate between two fundamental low-resolution narratives, neither of which can be completely accurate, because they can't encompass all the details. Obviously human beings have an individual element and a collective element—a group element, let's say. The question is, what story should be paramount?

This is how it looks to me: In the West, we have reasonably functional, reasonably free, remarkably productive, stable hierarchies that are open to consideration of the dispossessed that hierarchies generally create. Our societies are freer and functioning more effectively than any societies anywhere else in the world, and than any societies ever have. As far as I'm concerned—and I think there's good reason to assume this—it's because the fundamental low-resolution grand narrative that we've oriented ourselves around in the West is one of the sovereignty of the individual. And it's predicated on the idea that, all things considered, the best way for me to interact with someone else is individual to individual, and to react to that person as if they're part of the psychological process by which things we don't understand can yet be explored, and things that aren't properly organized in our society can be yet set right. The reason we're valuable as individuals, both with regard to our rights and our responsibilities, is because that's our essential purpose, and that's our nobility, and that's our function.

What's happening, as far as I'm concerned, in the universities in particular and spreading very rapidly out into the broader world—including the corporate world, much to what should be its chagrin—is a collectivist narrative. And, of course, there's some utility in a collectivist narrative, because we're all part of groups in different ways. But the collectivist narrative that I regard as politically correct is a strange pastiche of postmodernism and neo-Marxism, and its fundamental claim is that, no, you're not essentially an individual, you're essentially a member of a group. That group might be your ethnicity and it might be your sex and it might be your race, and it might be any of the endless numbers of other potential groups that you belong to, because you belong to many. And that you should be essentially categorized along with those who are like you on that dimension in that group — that's proposition number one.

Proposition number two is that the proper way to view the world is as a battleground between groups of different power. So, you define the groups first and then you assume that you view the individual from the group context, you view the battle between groups from the group context, and you view history itself as a consequence of nothing but the power of manoeuvres between different groups. That eliminates any consideration of the individual at a very fundamental level, and also any idea of free speech. Because if you're a collectivist at heart in this manner, there is no such thing as free speech. It isn't that it's debated by those on the radical Left and the rest of us; it's that in that formulation, there's no such thing as free speech because for an individualist, free speech is how you make sense of the world and reorganize society in a proper manner.

But for the radical Left type of collectivist that's associated with this viewpoint of political correctness, when you speak, all you're doing is playing a power game on behalf of your group. And there's nothing else that you *can* do, because that's all there is. And not only is that all there is in terms of who you are as an individual now, and how society should be viewed, it's also the fundamental narrative of history. For example, it's widely assumed in our universities now that the best way to conceptualize Western civilization is as an oppressive, male-dominated patriarchy, and that the best way to construe relationships between men and women across the centuries is one of oppression of women by men.

No hierarchy is without its tyranny. That's an axiomatic truth; people have recognized that for thousands of years. And hierarchies do tend toward tyranny, and they tend toward usurpation by people with power. But that only happens when they become corrupt. We have mechanisms in our society to stop hierarchies from becoming intolerably corrupt, and they actually work pretty well.

I would also point this out: don't be thinking that this is a debate about whether empathy is useful or not, or that the people on the "con" side of the argument are not empathetic. I know perfectly well, as I'm sure Mr. Fry does, that hierarchies tend to produce situations where people stack up at the bottom, and that the dispossessed in hierarchies need a political voice, which is the proper, necessary voice of the Left.

But that is not the same as proclaiming that the right level of analysis for our grand unifying narrative is that all of us are fundamentally to be identified by the groups we belong to, and to construe the entire world as the battleground between different forms of tyranny as a consequence of that group affiliation.

And to the degree that we play out that narrative, that won't be progress, believe me, and we certainly haven't seen that "progress" in the universities. We've seen situations like what happened at Wilfrid Laurier University instead. We won't see progress: what we'll return to is exactly the same kind of tribalism that characterizes the Left. Thank you.

RUDYARD GRIFFITHS: Thank you, Jordan. Michael Eric Dyson, your six minutes start now.

MICHAEL ERIC DYSON: Thank you very kindly. It's a wonderful opportunity to be here in Canada. Thank you so much. I'm going to stand here at the podium—I'm a preacher, and I *will* ask for an offering at the end of my presentation!

This is the swimsuit competition of the intellectual beauty pageant, so let me show you the curves of my thought. Oh my God, was that a politically incorrect statement I just made? How did we get to the point where the hijacking of the discourse on political correctness has become a kind of Manichean distinction between us and them? The abortive fantasy just presented is remarkable for both its clarity and yet the muddiness of the context from which it has emerged. What's interesting to me is that, when we look at the radical Left—I'm saying, where they at? I want to join them. They ain't running nothing. I'm from a country where a man stands up every day to tweet the moral mendacity of his viciousness into a nation he has turned into a psychic commode. Y'all got Justin; we got Donald.

So what's interesting, then, is that political correctness has transmogrified into a caricature of the Left. The Left came up with the term "political correctness," shall I remind you? We were tired of our excuses and our excesses and our exaggerations; we were willing to be self-critical in a way that I fear my *confrères*—my compatriots—are not. Don't take yourself too seriously—smile. Take yourself not seriously at all, but what you do, do with deadly seriousness. Now it has transmogrified into an attempt to characterize the radical Left. The radical Left is a metaphor, a symbol, an articulation. They don't exist; their numbers are too small. I'm on college campuses, I don't see much of them coming.

When I hear about identity politics, it amazes me. The collectivist identity politics? Uh, last time I checked, race was an invention from a dominant culture that wanted groups at their behest. The invention of race was driven by the demand of a dominant culture to subordinate others—patriarchy, right?

Patriarchy was the demand of men to have their exclusive vision presented. The beauty of feminism is that it's not going to resolve differences between men and women; it just says men don't automatically get the last word. Of course, in my career, they never did.

And so, identity politics has been generated as a *bête noire* of the Right, and yet the Right doesn't understand the degree to which identity has been foisted upon black people and brown people and people of colour from the very beginning, and on women and trans people. You think that I want to be part of a group that is constantly abhorred by people at Starbucks? I'm minding my own black business, walking down the street, I have group identity thrust upon me. They don't say, "Ah, aha, there goes a Negro—highly intelligent, articulate, verbose, capable of rhetorical fury at the drop of a hat—we should not interrogate him as to the *bona fides* of his legal status." No, they treat me as part of a group, and the problem—which our friends don't want to acknowledge—is that the hegemony, the dominance of that group, has been so vicious that it has denied us the opportunity to exist as individuals.

Individualism is the characteristic moment in modernity. Mr. Peterson is right. The development of the individual, however, is predicated upon notions of intelligence—Immanuel Kant and David Hume, and others. Philosophically, Descartes comes along, introducing knowledge into the fray, saying that knowledge is based upon a kind of reference to the golden intelligence, the reflective glass that one possesses. And yet it got rooted in the very ground of our existence.

So knowledge has a fleshly basis, and what I'm saying to you is that the knowledge that I bring as a person of colour makes a difference in my body, because I know what people think of me, and I know how they respond to me, and that ain't no theory.

Am I mad at trigger warnings? The only trigger warning I want is from a cop—Are you about to shoot me? Not funny in America, where young black people die repeatedly, unarmed, without provocation.

And so for me, identity politics is something very serious. And what's interesting about safe spaces—I hear about the university, I teach there. Look, if you have a safe space in your body, you don't need a safe space. Some of that is overblown, some of it is ridiculous, I understand. I believe that the classroom is a robust place for serious learning. I believe in the interrogation of knowledge based upon our mutual understanding of the edifying proposition of Enlightenment. At the same time, some people ain't as equal as others, so we have to understand the conditions under which they have emerged and in which they have been benighted and attacked by their own culture.

And I ain't seen nobody be a bigger snowflake than white men who complain: "Mommy, Mommy, they won't let us play and have everything we used to have under the old regime, where we were right, racist and supremacist and dominant and patriarchs and hated gays and lesbians and transsexuals." Yeah, you've got to share. This ain't your world; this is everybody's world.

And let me end by saying this: You remember that story from David Foster Wallace: "Two fish are going along and an older fish comes in the opposite direction. He says, 'Hello, boys, how's the water?' They swim on, they turn to each other: 'What the hell is water?'" Because when you're in it, you don't know it; when you're dominant, you don't know it. Nothing Keyser Söze said the devil did is more interesting than to make people believe he didn't exist. That's what white supremacy is.

RUDYARD GRIFFITHS: Thank you, Michael. Stephen, you're up. We're going to put six minutes on the clock.

STEPHEN FRY: I'll try to be as quick as possible, because if I miss that plane to London, I won't half hear the end of it from the bridegroom's mother.

Now, in agreeing to participate in this debate and stand on this side of the argument, I'm fully aware that many people who choose—incorrectly, in my view—to see this issue in terms of Left and Right, devalued and exploded terms as I think they are, will believe that I am betraying myself in such causes and values that I've espoused over the years. I've been given huge grief already, simply because I'm standing here next to Professor Peterson, which is the very reason that I am standing here in the first place.

I'm standing next to someone with whom I have differences, shall we say, in term of politics and all kinds of other things, precisely because I think all this has got to stop—this rage, resentment, hostility, intolerance; above all, this with-us-or-against-us certainty. A Grand Canyon has opened up in our world. The fissure, the crack, grows wider every day. Neither side can hear a word that the other shrieks; nor do they want to.

While these armies and propagandists in the culture wars clash, down below in the enormous space between the two sides, the people of the world try to get on with their lives, alternately baffled, bored, and betrayed by the horrible noises and explosions that echo all around. I think it's time for this toxic, binary, zero-sum madness to stop before we destroy ourselves.

I'd better nail my colours to the mast before I go any further than this; it's only polite to give you a sense of where I come from. All my adult life I have been what you might call a leftie, a soft leftie, a liberal of the most hand-wringing, milksop, milquetoast variety. Not a burning man-the-barricades socialist; not even really a progressive worth the name. I've been on marches, but I've never quite dared wave placards or banners. Am I a loathed member of that band, an sjw — a social justice warrior? I don't think highly of social *in*justice, I have to say, but I characterize myself mostly as a social justice *worrier*. My intellectual heroes, growing up, were Bertrand Russell and G. E. Moore, liberal thinkers, people like that, writers like E. M. Forster.

I believed, and I think I still do believe, in the sanctity of human relations, the primacy of the heart, and friendship and love and common interest. These are more personal interior beliefs than they are political exterior convictions, more a humanistic version of a religious impulse, I suppose. I trust in humanity, I believe in humanity — I think I do, despite all that has happened in the forty years of my adulthood.

I *am* soft, and I can easily be swept away by harder hearts and harder intellects. I'm sometimes surprised to be described as an activist, but over time I *have* energetically involved myself with what you might call causes. I grew up knowing that I was gay — well, in fact, from the very first I knew I was gay. I remember when I was born, looking up and saying, "That's the last time I'm going out one of those!"

I'm Jewish, so I have a natural, obvious horror of racism. Naturally I want racism, misogyny, homophobia, transphobia, xenophobia, bullying, bigotry, intolerance of all human kinds to end. That's surely a given amongst all of us. The question is how such a golden aim is to be achieved. My ultimate objection to political correctness is not that it combines so much of what I have spent a lifetime loathing and opposing: preachiness (with great respect), piety, self-righteousness, heresy-hunting, denunciation, shaming, assertion without evidence, accusation, inquisition, censoring. That's not why I'm incurring the wrath of my fellow liberals by standing on this side of the house.

My real objection is that I don't think political correctness *works*. I want to get to the golden hill, but I don't think that's the way to get there. I believe one of the greatest human failings is to prefer to be right than to be effective. And political correctness is always obsessed with how right it is, without thinking of how effective it might be.

I wouldn't class myself as a classical libertarian, but I do relish transgression, and I deeply and instinctively distrust conformity and orthodoxy. Progress is not achieved by preachers and guardians of morality but, to paraphrase Yevgeny Zamyatin, by madmen, hermits, heretics, dreamers, rebels, and skeptics.

I may be wrong—I hope to learn this evening. I really do think I may be wrong. I'm prepared to entertain the possibility that political correctness will bring us more tolerance and a better world. But I'm not sure.

I would like this quotation from my hero, Bertrand Russell, to hover over the evening: "One of the painful things about our time is that those who feel certainty are stupid, and those with any imagination and understanding are filled with doubt and indecision." Let doubt prevail.

RUDYARD GRIFFITHS: A great set of opening statements to set the scene. We're now going to go into a round of rebuttals, to allow each of our presenters three minutes to reflect on what they've heard, and to make some additional points. We'll do that in the same order that we had the opening statements. So, Michelle, you're up first. We'll put three minutes on the clock for you.

MICHELLE GOLDBERG: I think that the attempt to draw a dichotomy between individual rights and group rights is a little misleading. Traditionally, there have been large groups of people who have not been able to exercise their individual rights. And I think that a lot of the claims that are being made on behalf of what we "politically correct" types call marginalized groups are claims that people who have identities that have not traditionally been at the centre of our culture, or at the top of our hierarchies, have as much right to exercise their individual talents and realize their individual ambitions.

When we say that we want more women in power, or more voices of people of colour in the canon, or in the curriculum, or directing movies — all of these things are not, at least on my part, because I'm interested in some sort of very crude equity, but because there are a lot of people who have not traditionally been able to realize themselves as individuals. That's what the women's movement was; that's what the civil rights movement was; that's what the gay rights movement was; that's in some ways what the trans rights movement was. Far from a collectivist movement, this is a kind of classical liberalism pushed to its extreme. These are people saying, "I have the right to define my identity against the one that was collectively assigned to me."

Finally, I would say of a lot of the things that Stephen Fry said — and particularly his temperament — that we're probably in agreement. But this inquisition, this censoring. On the one hand I see where he's coming from, but I think it's a little bit virtual. I mean, who's really censoring you? I understand what it feels like to feel censored. I understand what it feels like to be on the wrong side of a Twitter mob, or get a lot of nasty comments. And that's a bad feeling. It's a counterproductive tactic, but it's not censorship.

And again, it's especially strange, coming from a country where the president is trying to levy additional postal rates on the owner of the *Washington Post*, in revenge for its reporting. And people who have kneeled to protest police brutality at football games have seen their careers explode. Or women who have challenged Mr. Peterson have been hounded by threats and trolls and misogynist invective.

RUDYARD GRIFFITHS: Jordan, please respond to what you've heard.

JORDAN PETERSON: Well, I guess I would like to set out a challenge in somewhat the same format as Mr. Fry did, to people on the moderate Left. I've studied totalitarianism for a very long time, both on the left and on the right in various forms. And I think we've done a pretty decent job of determining when right-wing beliefs become dangerous. I think that they become dangerous when they, and the people who stand on the right, evoke notions of racial superiority, or ethnic superiority, something like that. It's fairly easy — and necessary, I think — to draw a box around them and place them to one side. We've done a pretty good job of that.

What I fail to see happening on the left — and this is with regard to the sensible Left, because such a thing exists — is for the same thing to happen with regard to the radical leftists. So here's an open question: If it's not diversity, inclusivity, and equity as a triumvirate that marks out the too-excessive Left — and with equity defined, by the way, not as equality of opportunity, which is an absolutely laudable goal, but as equality of outcome, which is how it's defined — then exactly how do we demarcate the too-extreme Left? What do we do?

We say, "Well, there's no such thing as the too-extreme Left"? Well, that's certainly something that characterized much of intellectual thinking for the twentieth century, as our high-order intellectuals, especially in places like France, did everything they could to bend over backwards, to ignore absolutely everything that was happening in the catastrophic Left world in the Soviet Union and in Maoist China, not least. We've done a terrible job of determining how to demarcate what's useful from the Left from what's pathological.

And so, it's perfectly okay for someone to criticize my attempts to identify something like a boundary. We could say, diversity, inclusivity, and equity — especially equity, which is in fact equality of outcome, which is an absolutely abhorrent notion. If you know anything about history, you know that. And I'm perfectly willing to hear some reasonable alternatives. But what I hear continually from people on the left, as my opponents did, is to construe every argument that is possibly able to be construed on the axis of group identification. And to fail to help the rest of us differentiate the reasonable Left, which necessarily stands for the oppressed, from the pathological Left, which is capable of unbelievable destruction.

And what I see happening in the university campuses in particular, where the Left is absolutely predominant—and that's certainly not my imagination; that's well documented by perfectly reasonable people like Jonathan Haidt—is an absolute failure to make precisely that distinction. And I see the same thing echoed tonight.

RUDYARD GRIFFITHS: Michael, give us your rebuttal.

MICHAEL ERIC DYSON: I don't know what mythological collective Mr. Peterson refers to. I'm part of the Left. They're cantankerous. When they have a firing squad, it's usually in a semicircle.

Part of the skepticism of rationality was predicated upon the Enlightenment project, which says we're no longer going to be subordinate to superstition; we're going to think and we're going to think well.

Thomas Jefferson was one of the great arbiters of rationality, but he was also a man who was a slave-owner. How do you reconcile that? That's the complication I'm speaking about. That's not either/or; that's not a collective identity. Thomas Jefferson believed in a collective identity—that is, during the day. At night, he got some Luther Vandross songs, went out to the slave quarter, and engaged in sexual relations, and had many children with Sally Hemings. His loins trumped his logic.

And when Mr. Peterson talks about postmodernism, I don't know who he's talking about. I teach postmodernism; it's kind of fun. Jacques Derrida—just to say his name is beautiful. Michel Foucault talked about the insurrection of subjugated knowledge as people who had been marginalized now began to speak. The "subaltern," as Gayatri Spivak talks about it in postcolonial theory. The reason these people grew up and grew into existence and had a voice is because they had been denied. As Ms. Goldberg said, our group identity was foisted upon us; we were not seen as individuals. Babe Ruth, when he broke the home run record, didn't bat against all the best ballplayers; he batted against the best white ballplayers. When it's been rigged in your favour from the very beginning, it's hard for you to understand how much you've been rigged. You're born on third base, then you hit a triple.

And here we are, deriving our sense of identity from the very culture that we ignore. Look at the Indigenous names and the First Nations names—Toronto, Saskatchewan, Winnipeg, Tim Hortons.

But I'll tell you, there's an envy of the kind of freedom and liberty that people of colour and other minorities bring, because we bring the depth of knowledge in our body. There's a kind of jealousy of it. As the greatest living Canadian philosopher, Aubrey "Drake" Graham, says, "Jealousy is just love and hate at the same time."

I agree with Mr. Fry: we shouldn't be nasty and combative. And yet, I don't see nastiness and combativeness from people; I see them desiring to have their individual identities respected. When I get shot down for no other reason than I'm black, when I get categorized for no other reason than my colour, I am living in a culture that refuses to see me as a great individual.

STEPHEN FRY: It's interesting to hear that there really doesn't seem to be a problem, but yet, I think we all instinctively know that there is some kind of problem. There isn't censorship, of course not, in the way that there is in Russia. I've been to Russia and I have faced off with a deeply homophobic and unpleasant man, and there's political correctness in Russia. It's just political correctness on the right.

And that's what I grew up with, political correctness, which meant that you couldn't say certain things on television — you couldn't say "fuck," for example, on television, because it was incorrect to do so. And as always, the reason was that someone would appear and say, "I'm not shocked. Oh, of course, no, I'm not shocked, I'm not offended. I'm offended on behalf of others — young, impressionable plastic minds, the vulnerable."

And that's not good enough. See, I don't mind being called a faggot or a kike, or a mad person because I've got mental health issues. I don't mind people insulting me.

63

And people say, "Well, that's all right for you, Stephen, because you're strong." I don't feel particularly strong, and I don't know that I like being called a faggot and a kike, particularly, but I don't believe that the advances in my culture that have allowed me to be married — as I have now been for three years — to someone of my gender are a result of political correctness.

And maybe political correctness is actually just some sort of live trout, that the harder we squeeze it, the farther it goes away. And you will be saying, "I'm not talking about this; I'm talking about social justice," with which I agree, whether you want to call it identity politics, or the history of *your* people, or the history of *my* people. My people were slaves as well. The British were slaves of the Romans, and the Jews were slaves of the Egyptians — all human beings have been slaves at some point, and we all, in that sense, share that knowledge of how important it is to speak up.

But Russell Means, who was a friend of mine toward the end, who founded the American Indian Movement, said, "Oh for God's sake, call me an Indian, or a Lakota Sioux, or Russell. I don't care what you call me, it's how we're treated that matters." And so I'm really addressing a more popular idea. Also in Barrow, Alaska, an Iñupiat said, "Call me an Eskimo. It's obviously easier for you, because you keep mispronouncing Iñupiat."

I'll just end with a quick story. Gay rights came about in England because we slowly and persistently knocked on the door of people in power. We didn't shout, we didn't scream. People like Ian McKellen eventually got to see the prime minister. And when the Queen signed the Royal Assent for the bill allowing equality of marriage, she said, "Good lord, you know, I couldn't imagine this in 1953. Really is extraordinary, isn't it? Just wonderful!" and handed it over.

Now, that's a nice story, and I hope it's true. But it's nothing to do with political correctness; it's to do with human decency. It's that simple.

RUDYARD GRIFFITHS: Some great rebuttals there, and strong opening statements. Let's move now into the moderated cross-examination portion of this debate and get both sides engaging on some of the key issues here. I think what we've heard here is a bit of a tension — let's draw it out a bit more — between, on the one hand, the rights of groups to feel included and have the opportunity to define a group identity, and, on the other hand, a belief that there's something under threat when these groups are overly privileged through affirmative action or other outcome-oriented processes.

So, Michael, to start with you. Why isn't harm done to groups by privileging their group identity, whether it be a group identity of race or of gender, and not immediately treating them as individuals in the way that Jordan and Stephen would like you to see them first?

MICHAEL ERIC DYSON: Well, first of all, there was no arbitrary and random distinction that people of colour and other minority groups made. When I talked about the invention of race, the invention of gender, the invention of groupthink, that was not done by those groups that have been so named, as Ms. Goldberg said. So, first of all, you've got to acknowledge the historical evolution of that reality. The concept of group identity did not begin with them. It began with a group that didn't have to announce its identity. When you are in control, you don't have to announce who you are. Many white brothers and sisters don't see themselves as one among many ethnicities or groups. They see themselves as, "I'm just American, I'm Canadian, can't you be like us? Can't you transcend those narrow group identifications?"

And yet those group identifications have been imprinted upon them by the very people whose group power has now been challenged. Let's make no mistake about it: there's a challenge. I agree with Mr. Fry, in a kind of Neverland, about how sweet it would be to have a kingly and queenly metaphor about how it got resolved; that ain't the real deal, homie. In the real world, there's stuff at stake. What's at stake are bodies. What's at stake are people's lives. What's at stake is that people are still being lynched, killed. What's at stake is that people, because of their sexuality and their racial identity, are still being harmed.

So, what I'm suggesting to you is not that we are against being treated as individuals — that's what we're crying for. Please don't see me as a member of a group that you think is a thug, a nigger, a nihilist, a pathological person. See me as an individual who embodies the realities.

I'll end by saying this: what Michelle said is extremely important. The people who have individual rights did not have to fight for them in the same manner that people of colour and others have had to. When Mr. Fry talked about enslavement, he named them. Read Orlando Patterson's comparative history of race and slavery over twenty-eight civilizations. The Greeks did not have the same kind of slavery that Americans did. It was chattel slavery. In Greece you could buy back your freedom. You could teach the children of the people who enslaved you, and because of your display of prodigious intellect, you could secure your freedom. That was not the case in America; you were punished and killed for literacy.

My point is simply this: I am all for the celebration of broader identities, and I think that often those who are minorities, and others, are not celebrated to the degree that we are.

In America, we have the Confederate flag. We have white guys, mostly, in the South, but others as well, flying those Confederate flags that represent a part of the South that refused to cede its legitimate conquest at the hands of the North. They are waving that flag, not the American flag. They are not American; they are celebrating a secession, a move away from America. And a man named Colin Kaepernick, who is a football player, saying, "I want to bring beauty to that flag," has been denied opportunity.

So we have to really set the terms of debate in order before we proceed.

RUDYARD GRIFFITHS: Thanks, Michael, good point. Jordan, let's have you jump in on this idea of what you see as the pernicious danger of groupthink when it comes to ethnicity and gender. Why do you think that's one of the primal sins, in your view, of political correctness?

JORDAN PETERSON: Well, I think it's one of the primal sins of identity-politics players on the left *and* the right, just to be clear about that. Personally, since this has gotten personal at times, I'm no fan of the identitarian Right. I think that anybody who plays a conceptual game where group identity comes first and foremost risks an exacerbation of tribalism. It doesn't matter whether it's on the left or the right.

With regard to the idea of group rights, this is something we have fallen into terribly in Canada, not least because we've had to contend with the threat of Quebec separatism. The idea of group rights is extraordinarily problematic, because the obverse of the coin of individual rights is individual responsibilities. And you can hold an individual responsible, and an individual can *be* responsible, and so that's partly why individuals have rights.

But groups—how do you hold a group responsible? It's not a good idea to hold a group responsible. First of all, it flies in the face of the sort of justice systems that we've laid out in the West, which are essentially predicated first on the assumption of individual innocence, but also on the possibility of individual guilt—not group guilt. We saw what happened in the twentieth century, many, many times, when the idea of group guilt was able to get a foothold in the polity and in the justice system. It was absolutely catastrophic.

And so, okay, fine—group rights. How are you going to contend with the alternative to that, the opposite of that? Where's the group responsibility? How are you going to hold your groups responsible? "Well, we don't have to talk about that, because we're too concerned with rectifying historical injustices, hypothetical and otherwise." And that's certainly not to say that there wasn't any shortage of absolutely catastrophic historical injustices—that's not the point. The point is how you view the situation at the most fundamental level, and group rights are an absolute catastrophe in my opinion.

RUDYARD GRIFFITHS: Michelle, come in on that point. This is something you've written about—the idea that in identity politics the identity of the group is absolutely a valid part of the discourse, and individuals could and should be seen as participating in groups as they enter into the civic space.

MICHELLE GOLDBERG: I'm not sure that we necessarily have to analogize from the individual. The opposite of individual rights is individual responsibility, but I'm not sure that that analogy necessarily holds for groups.

One of the things that I think is complicated about this discussion is that we're talking about three very different cultural contexts, three different histories, three different kinds of legal regimes.

But in the United States, a huge part of our politics has been groups struggling for rights for their individual members: women in the United States seeking the right to reproductive control of their bodies; African Americans in the United States seeking redress from police brutality or discrimination or simply the tendency in America of white people to call the police whenever they see an

African American in a place where they don't think that they're supposed to be. I don't see how you can contend with any of those social problems if you see society as just an ocean of atomized individuals.

I don't think there's anything pernicious about people banding together on the basis of their common identity to seek redress for discrimination and exclusion. I think that that is everything that's best about our democracy; that *is* the definition of progress.

And so again, I keep stumbling on the idea that this is somehow tyrannical, or "that way lies Stalinism." And a lot of those people who are opposed to political correctness talk about the concept of "category creep," a concept that was originated by, I believe, an Australian academic. It's basically the failure to draw distinctions, so that you can't see the difference between, say, a KKK grand wizard and a conservative like, say, Ben Shapiro; or that you see everybody to your right as fascist, sexist, totalitarian, intolerable. And I think that is a real thing that happens, in part, because undergraduates often think in broad and slightly overwrought categories—I know I did when I was a kid, and maybe still do. But I hear a lot of category creep in the argument against political correctness, or against seeking group redress. The idea that "that way lies dehumanization."

RUDYARD GRIFFITHS: Let's have Stephen come in on this— this was part of your opening remarks. You're a "category creep," Stephen. Now respond to that.

STEPHEN FRY: I'm still very lost about why we aren't talking about political correctness; we're talking about politics — and that's fine. And I share exactly what you think about it. I'm not an enemy of identity politics per se. I can obviously see where it goes wrong and where it's annoying.

But let's be empirical about this: How well is it working for you in America at the moment? Not well at all; it really isn't. You can answer me in a moment.

The reason that Trump, and Brexit in Britain, and all kinds of nativists all over Europe are succeeding is not the triumph of the Right, it's the catastrophic failure of the Left. It's our fault.

My point is not that I've turned to the right or anything like that, or that I'm nice and fluffy and want everybody to be decent; I'm saying, "Fuck political correctness. Resist. Fight. If you have a point of view, fight it in the proper manner, using democracy as it should be, not channels of education, not language."

You know, the best move to play in chess is not the best chess move, it's the move your opponent least wants you to play. At the moment, you're being recruiting sergeants for the Right, by annoying and upsetting instead of either fighting or persuading.

But political correctness is a middle course that simply doesn't work. That's my point.

MICHAEL ERIC DYSON: Well, first of all, you said, "Be empirical." Now, as far as I know, the word "empirical" means that which can be verified or falsified through the senses.

STEPHEN FRY: Exactly.

MICHAEL ERIC DYSON: So if we look at it in an objective way, the reality is that people don't have equal access to the means to articulate the very moment you're talking about.

STEPHEN FRY: No, no, no. I'm talking about the empirical results of this political attitude.

MICHAEL ERIC DYSON: I understand that, but my point is simply this: I'm suggesting to you that people use the weapons at hand. Now, it was Abraham Joshua Heschel, the rabbi, who said that everybody's not guilty, but everybody's responsible. There's a distinction there.

Clearly, everybody is not guilty, but what's interesting is to look at the flip side. If you have benefited from three hundred years of holding people in servitude, thinking that you did it all on your own — "Why can't these people work harder? For three hundred years, you ain't had no job." So the reality is that for three hundred years, you hold people in abeyance. You hold them in subordination; you refuse to give them rights. Then all of a sudden you free them, and say, "You're now individuals" — not having the skills, not having —

JORDAN PETERSON: Who's this *you* that you're referring to?

MICHAEL ERIC DYSON: I'm talking about American society, first of all; I'm talking about the northern hemisphere; I'm talking about every society where enslavement has existed, but I'm speaking specifically of the repudiation of individual rights among people of colour in America, who were denied the opportunity to be individuals.

I obviously and ideally—and I think Michelle Goldberg does too—agree with the emphasis on individuals. What we're saying to you is that we have not been permitted to be individuals; we have not been permitted to exercise our individual autonomy and authority. And the refusal to recognize me as an individual means that when you roll up on me and I'm a twelve-year-old boy in a park, and you shoot first in ways you do to black kids that you don't do to white kids, you are not treating that person as an individual.

If we're living in a society where women are subject to aberrant forms of horrid, patriarchal sexist and misogynist behaviour, you are not acknowledging the centrality of the individuality of women; you are treating them according to a group dynamic.

I'll end by saying this: that great American philosopher, Beyoncé Knowles, said that it has been said that racism is so American that if you challenge racism, you look like you're challenging America. We are challenging inequality; we are challenging the refusal to see me as an individual. When we overcome that, we're all on an equal playing field.

RUDYARD GRIFFITHS: The pot is getting stirred here—I like it.

JORDAN PETERSON: Let's assume for a moment that I've benefited from my white privilege, okay?

MICHAEL ERIC DYSON: That's a good assumption.

JORDAN PETERSON: Yeah, well, that's what you would say. So let's get precise about this, okay?

MICHAEL ERIC DYSON: Mm-hmm, let's get precise.

JORDAN PETERSON: To what degree is my present level of attainment or achievement a consequence of my white privilege? Do you mean 5 percent? Do you mean 15 percent? Do you mean 25 percent? Do you mean 75 percent? And what do you propose I do about it?

How about a tax? How about a tax that's specialized for me so that I can account for my damn privilege, so that I can stop hearing about it?

Now, let's get precise about one other thing, okay? If we can agree — and we haven't — that the Left can go too far, which it clearly can, then how would my worthy opponents precisely define when the Left that they stand for has gone too far? You didn't like equity — equality of outcome — I think that's a great marker. But if you have a better suggestion and won't side-step the question, let's figure out how I can dispense with my white privilege, and you can tell me when the Left has gone too far, since they clearly can.

And that's what this debate is about — political correctness. It's about the Left going too far, and I think it's gone too far in many ways, and I'd like to figure out exactly how and when, so the reasonable Left could make its ascendance again and we could quit all this nonsense.

RUDYARD GRIFFITHS: Michelle, jump in.

MICHELLE GOLDBERG: Do you mind if I answer Stephen first? Stephen talked about how we got Trump, and that it was a failure of the Left.

I'm a journalist, as you know, and I went to a ton of Trump rallies during the campaign in different parts of the country. You're right: everywhere I went, I heard complaints about political correctness far more than I heard complaints about, say, NAFTA. But when you asked people what they meant by political correctness, they would complain that they called a woman they worked with "girl" and she got mad at them. And that you couldn't in public wonder aloud whether the president of the United States was really a Muslim. They didn't like that they couldn't make gay jokes anymore.

And so, on the one hand you're right. I think that when people have these kinds of prejudices and you try to suppress them, it can create a dangerous counter-reaction. But, again, to go back to the title of this debate, I also think that what they were reacting to — what they called political correctness — was the fact that they had to have this urbane black president who they felt talked down to them, which is really what they meant. I don't see a way around that, because as I said, that's progress.

As to the question of when the Left goes too far, to me it's pretty easy — violence and censorship. I'm against violence and I'm against censorship. Looking around the world right now, I understand that there is a problem of left-wing annoyance. There's a lot of ways in which random people on the internet, in particular, are able to swarm individuals and turn stray remarks into social media campaigns. This is often conflated with political correctness, and it's a bad phenomenon. I wish there was a way to put an end to it. But I don't think there is a way to put an end to it simply by having reasonable liberals or reasonable socialists denounce it. It's just a kind of awful phenomenon of modern life. And if you want to have a debate about whether social media is terrible for democracy, I will be on the "yea" side.

But, when you see actual fascism ascendant all over the world, the idea that the radical Left poses a greater threat than the radical Right strikes me as something that you can literally only believe if you spend your life on college campuses.

RUDYARD GRIFFITHS: Mike, I want to come to you on Jordan's point. How does he get an equal voice in this debate back, if it is implied that his participation brings with it this baggage of white privilege that doesn't allow him to see clearly the issues that are before us?

MICHAEL ERIC DYSON: But that is to be complicit in the very problem itself, terminologically. You're beginning at a point that's already productive and controversial. You're saying, How can he get his equality back? Who are you talking about? Jordan Peterson, trending number one on Twitter? Jordan Peterson, international bestseller? I want him to tweet something out about me and my book.

Jordan Peterson, this is what I'm saying to you: Why the rage, bro? You're doing well, but you're a mean, mad white man, and you're going to get us right. I have never seen so much whine and snowflaking. There's enough wine in here to start a vineyard. And what I'm saying to you, empirically and precisely, when you ask the question about white privilege, and ask it in the way that you did — dismissive, pseudo-scientific, non-empirical, and without justification — is that, first, the truth is that white privilege doesn't act according to quantifiable segments; it's about the degree to which we are willing, as a society, to grapple with the ideals of freedom, justice, and equality upon which it's based.

The second thing that was interesting to me was that you were talking about not having a collective identity. What do you call a nation? Are you Canadian? Are you Canadian by yourself? Are you an individual? Are you part of a group? When America formed its union, it did so in opposition to another group.

So the reality is that those who are part of group identities in politics deny the legitimacy and validity of those groups and the fact that they have been created thusly, and then have resentment against others. All I'm asking for is the opportunity.

The quotation you talk about — the difference between equality of outcome and equality of opportunity — that's a staid and retried argument, a hackneyed phrase, derived from the halcyon days of the debate over affirmative action. "Are you looking for outcomes that can be determined equally, or are you looking for opportunity?"

If you free a person after a whole long time of oppression and say, "Now you are free to survive," if they have no skills, if they have no quantifiable means of existence, what you have done is liberated them into oppression. And all I'm suggesting to you — as Lyndon Baines Johnson, one of our great presidents, said — is that if you start a man in a race a hundred years behind, it is awfully difficult to catch up.

So I don't think Jordan Peterson is suffering from anything except an exaggerated sense of entitlement and resentment, and his own privilege is invisible to him, and it's manifest with lethal intensity and ferocity right here on stage.

RUDYARD GRIFFITHS: Jordan, I'll let you respond to that if you will.

JORDAN PETERSON: Well, what I derived from that series of rebuttals is twofold: the first is that saying that the radical Left goes too far when they engage in violence is not a sufficient response by any stretch of the imagination, because there are sets of ideas in radical leftist thinking that led to the catastrophes of the twentieth century, and that was at the level of idea, not at the level of violent action. It's a very straightforward thing to say you're against violence; it's like being against poverty. Generically speaking, decent people are against poverty and violence. It doesn't address the issue in the least.

And with regard to my privilege or lack thereof, I'm not making the case that I haven't had advantages in my life, and disadvantages in my life, like most people. You don't know anything about my background or where I came from, but it doesn't matter to you, because fundamentally

I'm a "mean white man." That's a hell of a thing to say in a debate.

MICHAEL ERIC DYSON: Let me just say that the "mean white man" comment was not predicated upon my historical excavation of your past; it's based upon the evident vitriol with which you speak, and the denial of a sense of equanimity among combatants in an argument. So, I'm saying again, "you're a mean, mad white man," and the viciousness is evident.

RUDYARD GRIFFITHS: Okay, we should change tracks here. Let's talk about another big factor of the so-called politically correct movement right now, which is the #MeToo movement and the extent to which we've seen this resurgence, this awakening, around what had been a horrible series of systemic abuses and injustices toward women.

Some people, though, Michelle, would say that we're in a cultural panic now, that the pendulum has swung too far and that there is a dangerous overreaction going on, where people's rights, reputations, and due process have been thrown to the wind. How do you respond to that?

MICHELLE GOLDBERG: Well, first, people started saying that within two weeks of the first Harvey Weinstein stories breaking — the minute Harvey Weinstein and other men started actually losing their jobs. This was something quite new, that men with histories of really serious predatory behaviour were suddenly losing their jobs. Everybody had known about it for a long time and there had been a sort of implicit impunity, and suddenly that was taken away, and it created this cultural earthquake. And as soon as it did, it created a lot of anxiety: "What if this goes too far?"

The #MeToo movement was only a couple of months old when the *New York Times* started running columns from people saying, "Why can't I criticize #MeToo?" which they were doing in the newspaper.

Is due process important? Yes, obviously. But when you look at who has actually lost their jobs, who's actually lost their livelihoods, it's not on some McCarthyist rumour; it's people who took their dicks out at work; it's people who got tens of millions of dollars in settlements, and lost their jobs for four months, and now they're staging comebacks. Bill O'Reilly is about to get a TV show on a new network. The idea that men everywhere feel like they can't talk anymore, and everybody's walking on eggshells—maybe that's true in your offices, but it's not true where I live. And the #MeToo movement has been particularly active in media.

I don't know how many of you read about the "Shitty Media Men" list? A woman started an open-source document where women could list men in media that everybody knew about but nobody had ever done anything about. And it very quickly went public. But there was something disturbing in it. You don't like these anonymous accusations floating around. Most feminists I know, including myself, were kind of freaked out by it and thought it was unfair to have people's reputations held up like this.

But, if you look at what happened to the men on the list…nothing. They still have their jobs. I know men on that list; I work with men on that list. The people in media who have actually lost their jobs and lost their careers have done so for extremely serious misbehaviour, documented by multiple women who had corroborating witnesses.

I understand this anxiety that relations between men and women are changing; of course, that causes a lot of cultural anxiety. But I don't know that it's rooted in anything real.

RUDYARD GRIFFITHS: I'm going to bring Stephen in here and get his view on this. Are we in a cultural panic? Is the response commensurate with the moment?

STEPHEN FRY: I'm very confused by this. Of course I recognized the bestiality of Weinstein and the monstrosity of his behaviour, and it was shocking to me. I actually worked for him — script-doctoring, as it's called — and I never had the bathroom towel, but for pretty obvious reasons. But it's grotesque, and I can't imagine how vile it must be — such a powerful man. We used to play a game at the Cannes Film Festival in his years of power. We would walk from one hotel at the end all the way up to the Palais des Festivals. You would get ten points every time you heard the word "Harvey." Usually, in a ten-minute walk, you'd have three hundred points, because it was, "Yeah, Harvey's got the script…Harvey's got it…Yeah, I've got a meeting with Harvey at the Majestic in the afternoon." He was immensely powerful, and I think it's obvious that someone in that position abusing and threatening and hindering the livelihood of women is grotesque in the extreme.

But I have to tell you, there is genuine feeling amongst many people I know that, "Shhh," we can't speak our minds, that we can't actually speak to the true nuance, the true depth of sexual romantic feeling between men and women. It's not a subject I'm absolutely expert on, but it counts between men and men as well, though I know that when it's men and men, you might say, "Well, that's different, because women have had a different experience in history," and I don't want to enter that particular field.

But I would say that there is real fear. In my business, where this all started — show business, acting, and so on — people are rather afraid to speak about a piece of publicity that's come out, or a statement that's been made. You just go, "Yeah, absolutely," and wait for the people to leave the room before you can speak honestly with your friends.

I've never experienced that in my entire sixty years on this planet, this feeling that — and I'm not characterizing feminists as East German — but it's like the Stasi listening: you'd better be careful; they're listening. And that's a genuine feeling. I'm saying that with my hand on my heart. I'm not saying it to make a point other than the fact that it's true and it's worrying. But the sexual misadventure and horror experience is worrying too; so there are two worries, and they're not solved.

RUDYARD GRIFFITHS: Let's bring Jordan in on this, because he's written and commented about it a lot. But Stephen, thank you for that.

JORDAN PETERSON: Well, I think I'm going to point out two things again. The first is that my question about when the Left goes too far *still* hasn't been answered. And the second is that it's conceivable that I am a mean man — maybe I'm meaner than some people, and not as mean as others (although I think that's probably more the case). But I would say that the fact that race got dragged into that particular comment is a better exemplar of what the hell I think is wrong with the politically correct Left than anything else that could have possibly happened.

MICHAEL ERIC DYSON: Imagine the hurt, the anxiety, the insult that you might genuinely feel, according to what I felt was an appropriate comment of description at the moment of its expression. But imagine now, those hurt feelings and —

JORDAN PETERSON: I'm not hurt.

MICHAEL ERIC DYSON: Okay, you feel great! You feel great about it!

JORDAN PETERSON: That's really different. I'm not a victim. I'm not hurt. I'm appalled.

MICHAEL ERIC DYSON: You're not hurt, okay. You wouldn't be a victim. So what's interesting is that whatever non-traditional feelings of empathy you endure at this particular point, imagine, then, the horrors that so many other "others" have had to put up with for so long, when they are refused an acknowledgement of their humanity.

Now, I take your point seriously. What I'm saying to you is that, when you said you were upset that I added the element of race when I said, "mean, mad white man," what's interesting is that you may have felt that you were being ascribed a group identity to which you do not subscribe. You may have felt that you were being unfairly judged according to your particular race. You may have felt that your individual identity was being besmirched by my rather careless characterization of you. All of that qualifies as a legitimate response to me. But it also speaks to the point we've been trying to make about the refusal to see our individual existence, as women, as people of colour, as First Nations people and the like.

My point simply has been: the reason I talked about race in that particular characterization is because there's a particular way in which I have come to a city—I don't know if there are a lot of black people out here...I'm not sure. But I constantly come to places and spaces that are not my natural habitat—other than for intellectual engagement and the love and the fury of rhetorical engagement, yes. But I often go into hostile spaces, where people will not vote in favour of my particular viewpoint, because I'm interested as an individual in breaking down barriers so that people can understand just how complicated it is.

So, what I'm saying to you is that I would invite you, in terms of the surrender of your privilege—to give you a specific response—to come with me to a black Baptist church. Come with me to a historically black college; come with me to an Indigenous or First Nations community, where we're able to engage in some lovely conversation, but also to listen and hear.

And when I added race to that, I was talking about people's historical inability to acknowledge others' pains equally to the ones that they are presently enduring.

So, as a human being, I love you, my brother, but I stand by my comment.

JORDAN PETERSON: Well, I've seen the sorts of things that you're talking about. I happen to be an honorary member of an Indigenous family, so don't tell me about what I should go see with regard to oppression. You actually don't know anything about me.

MICHAEL ERIC DYSON: You asked me a question, I gave you a response.

JORDAN PETERSON: You gave me a generic response, a generic race-based response.

MICHAEL ERIC DYSON: It's tailored toward you. Jordan Peterson, I would like for you to come with me, Michael Eric Dyson, to a black Baptist church. You've been to one of those?

JORDAN PETERSON: I would be happy to do that, but—

MICHAEL ERIC DYSON: Okay, all right, I'm going to hook you up.

RUDYARD GRIFFITHS: One more quick round, then we're going to go to closing statements. Stephen Fry, a generation from now, looking back on this debate, are we not going to see this so-called politically correct movement in the same way that we now understand the positive contributions of, say, the civil rights movement? That was a movement that advanced a series of ideas about human dignity to people who previously didn't have that dignity. We're now having another debate, another social debate, about different groups and communities—we're trying to convey a sense of new dignity to them. Why won't this be looked back upon as something positive, a generation from now?

STEPHEN FRY: I think people will look back on this debate and wonder why political correctness wasn't discussed.

It's interesting to hear talk about race and about gender and about equality, and it's something that I've thought about a lot and I can learn a great deal about, but that's not why I came to this debate. I was interested in what I've always been interested in: the suppression of language and thought, the closing down, the rationalist idea that seems beguiling, that if you limit people's language, you may somehow teach them a different way of thinking, something that delighted the inventors of George Orwell's Newspeak, for example.

And it seems to me that it's just implausible, that it doesn't work. And that's what I mean by empirical. It doesn't stand an empirical test; it isn't experientially validated, as we see from the political landscape now and I worry that we may in the future.

So, I'm sort of disappointed that the subject has just revolved around academia, which was predictable, because that's the sort of crucible in which these elements are mixed. But even more disappointed that really, I haven't heard from Michelle or from Professor Dyson as to what they think political correctness is. Because what they've talked about is basically saying, "Progress, in our view, is progress." Well, I agree. So it is. And good on progress!

But how is it that what we call political correctness you call progress? That's what you're supposed to be arguing. I want to know what you mean by political correctness.

MICHELLE GOLDBERG: A few months ago, when you, Rudyard, contacted me and asked if I wanted to participate in a debate about identity politics and presented me with this resolution, I said there are a lot of things that people call political correctness that I'm not going to defend. But then I realized who I would be debating, and saw that there were a lot of things that you, Jordan Peterson, call political correctness that I call progress. And to some extent, you too, Stephen Fry. You know, when you talk about it being outrageous—or not "outrageous"; I won't put words into your mouth—but that we shouldn't be tearing down statues of notorious racists; that we should just instead be throwing eggs at them. Those sorts of things, if you call them political correctness, I call them progress.

Now, as for this feeling of being silenced, which I understand, although it seems very vague: you are not quite putting your finger on who is silencing you, except for a vague fear that if you say something untoward, you're going to be the subject of —

STEPHEN FRY: Shaming.

MICHELLE GOLDBERG: Shaming, but by who? By the internet?

STEPHEN FRY: I'm not going to tell you the names. That's the whole point: I'm scared. It's a culture of fear.

MICHELLE GOLDBERG: I understand there's that element of fear. What I'm saying is that it's a feeling that is the intangible result of —

STEPHEN FRY: Okay, but we've all seen the sort of show trial thing, where the person then apologizes — "I have so much to learn about sexual politics, I am really sorry." Signed... the lawyer. Crossed out... the name of the person.

The real mistake of our Left is that we underestimate the Right. The Right isn't as stupid as we'd like them to be. If only they were. If only they weren't so cunning, so sly, so smart, so aware of our shortcomings.

And I fear that political correctness is a weapon that they value; that the more we tell the world how people should be treated — how language should be treated, what words are acceptable, what attitudes are acceptable, what HR is going to tell you in a long bullet-pointed list about how you look at people — all of this is meat and drink to bad people, to malefactors, to bad actors. I'm not including myself as one of those "bad actors" in that sense; I mean "bad actors" in the other sense!

MICHELLE GOLDBERG: There are a lot of ways in which I agree with you, although, to turn it back on you, I'd like to hear you say what are the words that have fallen into disrepute that you think we should be resurrecting. To me, this is an area of hotly contested social change right now, where a lot of people feel —

STEPHEN FRY: I have to say this about words that have gone into disuse: it's very often phrases, jargonistic slogans, "heteronormative," "cisgendered," those kind of things. They're just an insult. Imagine you're a young student arriving at university and someone's bombarding you with this preposterous hermeneutical nonsense from misread textbooks and misread Foucault, if I may say — misread Derrida, and so on. Because, you know, I was at Cambridge doing literature. We had our French phase, and there's value in that. It's an interesting game.

I think I'll just say that the ghost hovering over for me is a letter Oscar Wilde wrote, and he said to Bosie, his lover, "The fact that you didn't get the degree is nothing, but you never acquired what is sometimes called the Oxford manner." And I'll say to that, the university manner. Oscar said, "I take that to mean the ability to play gracefully with ideas." I think that's disappearing from our culture, and I think it's a terrible thing.

MICHAEL ERIC DYSON: It's hard to be the self-deprecating Englishman.

STEPHEN FRY: You've *no* idea.

MICHAEL ERIC DYSON: I got a pretty good idea here today. All of us have studied history, but what's interesting is that I don't recall these debates about political correctness happening when people who were in power were in absolute power, unquestioned power.

Political correctness becomes an issue when people who used to have power, or who still have power but think they don't, get challenged on just a little bit of what they have and don't want to share — toys in the sandlot of life. So, all of a sudden it becomes a kind of exaggerated grievance.

Now, the things you named — the bullet-points and the cisgender and the heteronormativity and the heteropatriarchy and the capitalist resurgence and the insurrection of subjugated knowledges, to give Foucault some more love, or the Derridean deconstruction — all that stuff; the French phase is still going on with the french fries in America. What's interesting is that I didn't hear many complaints of political correctness at the height of the dominance of one group or another, but when Martin Luther King Jr., who argued for group identity, as a black person, to provide an opportunity for individual black people to come to the fore, they began to make that claim.

Now, they didn't call it political correctness. "You're siding with those who are against free speech; you're siding with those who don't want me as a white person to be recognized in my humanity." And what I mean by political correctness is the kind of politics of *ressentiment* that are articulated by various holders of power at certain levels, at various levels.

One of the beautiful things about Foucault is that he said power breaks out everywhere. I would think a person who is critical of political correctness like you would appreciate this. As opposed to Max Weber, who said that power is over there in a hierarchical structure, where subordination is the demand, Foucault said, "No, power breaks out even among people who are disempowered." So you can hurt somebody in your own community.

What's more politically incorrect than a black Baptist preacher identifying with a first-century Palestinian Jew and still loving atheists? What's more politically incorrect than a black intellectual going on Bill Maher and defending his ability to continue to have his show, despite using the N-word.

I, sir, believe in a politically incorrect version of the world. When I go as a black Baptist preacher to chastise my fellow believers about their homophobia, that goes over like a brick cloud. When I come into arenas like this, I understand that my back is up against the wall, but—

STEPHEN FRY: Then come and sit over here!

MICHAEL ERIC DYSON: So, what's interesting is that when we look at what is seen as political correctness in our societies—in a free Canadian society, in a free American society—to me it has been a massive jumble that has been carved out of the politics of resentment that powers once held are no longer held; freedoms once exercised absolutely must now be shared.

So I am in agreement with both of the gentlemen to my right, who believe that political correctness has been a scourge, but not necessarily the way you think. I think it's been a scourge because those who have been the deployers of power and the beneficiaries of privilege have failed to recognize their particular way. And at the end of the day, I think that those of us who are free citizens of this country, and of America, should figure out ways to respect the humanity of the other, to respect the individual existence of the other, and also respect the fact that barriers have been placed upon particular groups that have prevented them from flourishing. That's all I mean by political correctness.

RUDYARD GRIFFITHS: Before we go to closing statements, I'm going to give the final words on this topic to Michelle and then you, Jordan.

MICHELLE GOLDBERG: I think part of the frustration here is that both of you have radically different ideas of what we're talking about when we talk about political correctness. It seems to me that when you, Stephen, are talking about political correctness, you mean the kind of feeling of anxiety that a lot of people feel because we all live now in this terrible crowd-sourced panopticon that makes you worry that any straight phrase you utter might be used to defame you, right?

I think that a lot of people feel that anxiety. I disagree that that is something that is being solely perpetrated against insouciant Oscar Wildean figures by a censorious left-wing core, because it's coming from all directions. This phenomenon — which sucks — is all over the place. I get it when I write something critical of the way that the Israel Defense Forces behaved in Gaza. It's coming at everyone, and I think that when it comes at a certain sort of figure and there's a certain set of complaints, and you feel unjustly criticized, and you feel silenced — which is really different from *being* silenced — you call it political correctness.

I would also like the culture to be more freewheeling. You're not going to get the Left to put an end to this, because it is much more of a mob social media phenomenon than it is some diktat coming from on high. Really, the only way to break through it is to say what you're afraid to say, right? That's the only way to pop this bubble, to end this anxiety, or at least diffuse it a little bit.

What I hear Mr. Peterson talking about as political correctness is something much broader, and much more fundamental to social change. And you want me to define — or one of us to talk about when the Left goes too far. And I certainly don't want to be a woman putting words in your mouth, but if I hear you correctly, what you're saying is that you want me to renounce Marxist categories, or to —

JORDAN PETERSON: It's up to you. I just want you to *do* it. I want you to define when the Left goes too far. You can do it any way you want.

MICHELLE GOLDBERG: I think that the Left goes too far when it is violent or censorious, when it tries to shut people down, or "no-platform" them, or when it acts violently. I'm not sure what you expect beyond that.

JORDAN PETERSON: Something deeper.

MICHELLE GOLDBERG: Something deeper? How?

JORDAN PETERSON: I'd like you to contend with the set of left-wing ideas that produced all the left-wing pathologies of the twentieth century, and to define how you think standard left-wing thinking, which has a valuable place, goes too far, since it obviously does.

MICHAEL ERIC DYSON: Has the Right gone too far?

JORDAN PETERSON: Of course the Right has gone too far.

MICHAEL ERIC DYSON: How? Tell us how?

JORDAN PETERSON: Well, how about Auschwitz?

MICHAEL ERIC DYSON: What else? More recently, what has gone wrong with the Right?

STEPHEN FRY: Charlottesville?

JORDAN PETERSON: Look, I don't like identity-politics players at all. I don't care whether they're on the left or the right. I've been lecturing about right-wing extremism for thirty years. I'm no fan of the Right, despite the fact that the Left would like to paint me that way, because it's more convenient for them.

MICHAEL ERIC DYSON: How has the Right gone too far recently?

JORDAN PETERSON: It's threatening to go too far in identitarian Europe, that's for sure. It's gone too far in Charlottesville; it went too far in Norway. How long a list do you want? And why am I required to produce that? To show you that I don't like the identitarian Right?

MICHAEL ERIC DYSON: You asked me, so I just thought I'd ask you.

JORDAN PETERSON: I was actually asking you a question. So your assumption is somehow that I must be on the side of the Right. Look, the Right hasn't occupied the humanities and the social sciences. It's as simple as that for me. If they had, I'd be objecting to them.

MICHAEL ERIC DYSON: Say that again, I didn't hear.

JORDAN PETERSON: The Right has not occupied the social sciences and the humanities, and the Left clearly has—the statistical evidence for that is overwhelming.

MICHAEL ERIC DYSON: So, what about IQ testing in terms of genetic inheritance?

JORDAN PETERSON: We're here to talk about political correctness, and we've done a damn poor job of it.

MICHAEL ERIC DYSON: Oh, I see. I gave you an example and you can't answer. Okay, all right.

RUDYARD GRIFFITHS: Let's all redeem ourselves with our closing statements. I'm going to put three minutes on the clock, and we're going to go in the reverse order of the opening. So, Stephen, you're up first.

STEPHEN FRY: I've been fascinated by this conversation. There's been an enormous clash of cultures in the conversation. We've had classic, if I can call it that, huckstering, snake-oil pulpit talk. It's a mode of discourse, a rhetorical style that I find endlessly refreshing and vivifying. But I'm not sure that we actually focused on the point in question. And my objection has always been toward orthodoxies — I'm a heterodox and a contrarian, and I can't help myself. And I think there's been an underestimation of the fact that language does affect people. It does make the young, in particular, very anxious, as they're starting out on their education, or their work careers. It makes them very angry, very upset, very alienated to feel that they don't know anymore how to operate in the world, how to engage in relationships, how to think honestly. So they accrete more and more to their own mini-groups. And I think that's dangerous and unhappy for society. I think it's reflected in a paucity of cinema and literature and art, and the culture generally. There's a fear that's pervading it. And while people can talk to academics and they'll say, "You should come and see our lessons; our lectures are open and free, and ideas are exchanged," I'm sure that's true, but I don't think we should underestimate how much this feeling is prevalent in the culture.

It's a strange paradox that the liberals are illiberal in their demand for liberality. They are exclusive in their demand for inclusivity. They are homogenous in their demand for heterogeneity. They are somehow un-diverse in their call for diversity — you can be diverse, but not diverse in your opinions and in your language and in your behaviour. And that's a terrible pity.

I'm sorry that it got a bit heated in places, because I was hoping it wouldn't. I was hoping it would be a shining example of how people of all different kinds of political outlooks can speak with humour and wit and a lightness of touch. As G. K. Chesterton said, "Angels can fly because they take themselves lightly."

And I think it's very important for us, who are privileged — all four of us, privileged to be here, to be asked to be here — to take ourselves a little bit more lightly, not to be too earnest, too pompous, too serious. And not to be too certain.

It's a time, I think, for really engaging, emotionally fulfilling, passionate and positive doubt. That's what I would urge. Thank you.

RUDYARD GRIFFITHS: Michael, I'm going to put three minutes on the clock for you.

MICHAEL ERIC DYSON: Thank you so much for that compliment, Brother Fry. I'm used to not exclusively white men who see black intelligence articulated at a certain level feeling a kind of condescension. A kind of verbal facility is automatically assumed to be a kind of hucksterism and snake-oil salesmanship. I've seen that. I get it. I get hate letters every day from white brothers and sisters who are mad I'm teaching their children. "You are just trying to co-opt our children; you are trying to corrupt them." Yes, I'm trying to corrupt them so that they will be uncorrupted by the corruptibility that they've inherited from a society that refuses to see all people as human beings.

The death threats I have received constantly for simply trying to speak my mind...it's not about a politically correct society that is open-minded and that has some consternation about my ability to speak. I'm getting real, live—you want empirical—death threats that talk about killing me, setting up to hurt me and harm me, simply because I choose to speak my mind.

I agree with my *confrères* and my compatriots that we should argue against the vicious limitations and recursions against speech. I believe that everybody has the right to be able to articulate themselves. And the enormous privilege we have to come to a space like this means that we have that privilege and we should be responsible for it.

No matter where we go from here, me and Brother Peterson will go to a black Baptist church. I'm going to hold him to that; he said it on national TV. We're going to go to a black Baptist church and have an enlightening conversation about the need for us to engage not only in reciprocal and mutual edification but in criticism—even hard and tough criticism. But in a way that speaks to the needs and interests of those who don't usually get on

TV, whose voices are not usually amplified, whose ideas are not usually taken seriously. And when they get to the upper echelons of the ability of a society to express themselves, they are equally subject to vicious recrimination and hurtful resistance.

There's an old story about the pig and the chicken going down the street and saying, "Let's have breakfast." The chicken just has to give up an egg; the pig has to give up his ass in order to make breakfast. We have often been the pigs, giving up our asses to make breakfast. Let's start sharing them asses with everybody else. Thank you.

JORDAN PETERSON: I'm not here to claim that there's no such thing as oppression, unfairness, brutality, discrimination, unfair use of power — all of those. Anyone with any sense knows that hierarchical structures tilt toward tyranny, and that we have to be constantly wakeful to ensure that all they are isn't just power and tyranny.

It's interesting to hear Foucault referred to; it's unfortunate, but it's interesting, because Foucault, like his French intellectual *confrères*, essentially believed that the only basis upon which hierarchies were established is power. And that's part of this pernicious politically correct doctrine that I've been speaking about. When a hierarchy becomes corrupt, then the only way to ascend it is to exercise power — that's essentially the definition of a tyranny.

But that doesn't mean the imperfect hierarchies that we have constructed in our relatively free countries don't at least tilt somewhat toward competence and ability, as evidenced by the staggering achievements of civilization that we've managed to produce. It doesn't mean that the appropriate way of diagnosing them is to assume, without reservation, unidimensionally, that they're all about power, and as a consequence, that everyone who occupies any position within them is a tyrant or a tyrant in the making. And that is certainly the fundamental claim of someone like Foucault. And it's part and parcel of this ideological catastrophe that is political correctness.

I'm not here to argue against progress. I'm not here to argue against equality of opportunity. Anyone with any sense understands that, even if you're selfish, you're best served by allowing yourself access to the multiplicitous talents of everyone; and to discriminate against them for arbitrary reasons unrelated to their competences is abhorrent. That has nothing to do with the issue at hand. It isn't that good things haven't happened in the past and shouldn't continue to happen — that's not the point. The point is the point my compatriot Fry has made, which is: well, we can agree on the catastrophe and we can agree on the historical inequity, but there's no way I'm going to agree that political correctness is the way to address any of that. And there's plenty of evidence to the contrary, some of which I would say was displayed quite clearly tonight.

MICHELLE GOLDBERG: I think that one of the irresolvable issues that we're all coming up against is the role of feelings, right? Stephen Fry has asked us to recognize and empathize with his feeling of being silenced, of being threatened, and I do. I get it. I feel it sometimes too in my columns. I hate it when I write something that then gets an irate Twitter mob after me. But if, say, I stood up here and said: recognize how threatened so many women feel when one of the bestselling and most prominent intellectuals in the world right now says in an interview that maybe the #MeToo movement has shown that this whole experiment of men and women working together is just not working? Or that maybe if women don't want the workplace to be sexualized, they shouldn't be allowed to wear makeup?

JORDAN PETERSON: I didn't say that.

MICHELLE GOLDBERG: It was in a VICE interview. Google it.

JORDAN PETERSON: I didn't say that.

MICHELLE GOLDBERG: If I say that I feel threatened, then I'm being "politically correct" and "hysterical." So much of the debate about political correctness, so much of the condemnation of political correctness, is about people saying, "Respect my feelings, or accommodate my feelings." And to some extent we can accommodate everyone's feelings.

But there's one group that really does think its feelings should be accommodated, and that is what we keep coming up against. There is a group of people—and to some extent I'm part of it—that feels uniquely that our feelings of being silenced, marginalized, and censored need to take primacy; that we can sneer when these *other* groups ask us to take seriously their feelings of being threatened, or their feelings of being marginalized. Then we call those demands "political correctness."

Finally, there's a fair amount of research that people become more close-minded, more tribal, when they feel threatened, when they feel that their group identity is at stake. And so, as much as you want to blame the Left for the rise of the Right, I think that the rise of the Right — the rise of people who are questioning the fundamental ideal of pluralistic liberal democracy — the more *those* views are mainstreamed, the more people are going to shut down in response, because people are *really* scared.

RUDYARD GRIFFITHS: Thank you. Well, first of all, on behalf of all the debaters, we want to thank the audience. You were engaged, you were mostly civil — and not-so-civil in ways that I think we enjoyed. So on behalf of the debaters, thank you, audience. This was a challenging topic and you did a great job.

Also a big thank you to our debaters. It's one thing to give regular speeches, as you all do, but it's a very different thing to come on a stage in front of a live audience and a large television audience and have your ideas contested in real time. So to all four of you, thank you for accepting our invitation to come here tonight.

A few final notes: first, thank you to the Aurea Foundation and the Munk family for once again convening us here at Roy Thomson Hall. We're going to do it all again this coming autumn.

All of you here in the hall have a ballot — you can vote on your way out. We'll have those results for you soon. Let's just quickly review where your opinion stood at the beginning of tonight's contest. On the motion, "Be it resolved, what you call political correctness, I call progress," 36 percent agreed, 64 percent disagreed. And again, we saw a large percentage of you willing to change your mind — 87 percent. So let's see how tonight's cut and thrust affected your voting.

Summary: The pre-debate vote was 36 percent in favour of the resolution, 64 percent against it. The final vote showed 30 percent in favour of the motion and 70 percent against. Given that more of the voters shifted to the team against the resolution, the victory goes to Stephen Fry and Jordan Peterson.

Post-Debate Interviews with Moderator
Rudyard Griffiths

STEPHEN FRY AND JORDAN PETERSON IN CONVERSATION WITH RUDYARD GRIFFITHS

RUDYARD GRIFFITHS: Gentlemen, thank you. We'd like to get your reactions to the debate. We'll start with you, Jordan. There were some heated moments out there. Did that surprise you, the exchanges that you had with Michael Eric Dyson?

JORDAN PETERSON: Well, I suppose it probably did. It just didn't seem like a very good tactical move, you know. I stand by what I said: I don't see any reason at all for my racial identity to be dragged into the discussion, independent of my personality proclivity.

As I just said to Mr. Fry here, it was a pleasure sharing the stage with him. I've rarely heard anyone ever deliver their convictions with such a remarkable sense of passion and wit and forbearance and erudition—it was really something.

RUDYARD GRIFFITHS: And Stephen, a challenging debate, because in a sense we were trying to mesh two different world views here, one focused more on identity politics, group identity. You, in a sense, had an argument really more about the larger culture itself and the tenor and tone of the conversation.

STEPHEN FRY: Yes, I worried that I was being a little scatter-gun really, but scattergun and too specific — that I had just taken very literally the popular idea of political correct-ness as being a kind of control of language and a shutting down of certain phrases, or an introduction of others. And the kind of day-to-day human resource departments of corporations and that sort of thing. So I was slightly disappointed that it just became a debate about race and about gender and so on. But that was natural, I guess. And the fact is that I'm still a leftie, but a soft one.

RUDYARD GRIFFITHS: You're not too soft!

STEPHEN FRY: I'm flabby and squashy in every sense. And I realize that that's not a political point of view; it is a personal one.

RUDYARD GRIFFITHS: Right.

STEPHEN FRY: And the gap between the personal and the political, which is a space you're obviously very interested in as a psychologist, is one that is rarely explored. People are either so personal that it has no application in the outside world and the organization of human affairs. Or, they're so political and so focused on structure and the distinction between hierarchies and networks and so on, that they forget the individual. And that's the space in which the impassioned liberal lives, and it's not easy to do, because you often do sound rather wet. And I'm aware that I did. But I enjoyed it.

RUDYARD GRIFFITHS: Well, thank you for coming. Just finally, before I free you both to a well-earned drink, is there anything you felt was left unsaid, Jordan? Any point that you wanted to make that you didn't feel you had the time or the opportunity for?

JORDAN PETERSON: No, I don't think so. I said my piece.

RUDYARD GRIFFITHS: Same question to you, Stephen?

STEPHEN FRY: No, I think I got everything across. I mean, there's so much you can talk about in that field, and I just wanted to leave the point that I do want—like everybody, it's a no-brainer—we want the world to be fairer, juster, sweeter, kinder. But it's a question of how you get there, and I felt that wasn't really addressed.

RUDYARD GRIFFITHS: Well, gentlemen, thank you both very much.

MICHAEL ERIC DYSON AND MICHELLE GOLDBERG
IN CONVERSATION WITH RUDYARD GRIFFITHS

RUDYARD GRIFFITHS: We now have Michael Eric Dyson and Michelle Goldberg coming in to give their reactions to the debate.

So, Michael and Michelle, thank you for being part of this.

MICHELLE GOLDBERG: Thank you.

RUDYARD GRIFFITHS: Political correctness is a complicated subject; it's got a lot of different moving pieces and elements. I think we addressed some of the constituent parts. Maybe we can start with you, Michelle. Was there something that you wanted to say on stage that we didn't have the time or the opportunity for?

MICHELLE GOLDBERG: Well, the only thing I can think of is that I wish we could have drilled down a little bit more into the gender piece of this, particularly with Mr. Peterson, and the range of feminist progress that he considers political correctness. I think part of the frustration is that he and Stephen Fry were talking about and defending a fairly discrete set of ideas with some overlap. And one of the difficult things about political correctness is that it's a slippery term that's deployed to talk about a whole range of phenomena.

RUDYARD GRIFFITHS: Yes, and to close down conversation and open up conversation. How did you feel, Michael? There were some points there of sharp exchange. We appreciate that at the Munk Debates; this is not a place for shrinking wallflowers. Do you have any unsaid thoughts, anything that you want to put a point on now?

MICHAEL ERIC DYSON: Well, I think you have to hold people intellectually accountable, and for Mr. Peterson to deny to Michelle some of the things that he has said, and to present himself in a certain way, without saying some of the abhorrent things he has said about women and other minorities, demands an engaged response to him.

The frustration expressed by Mr. Fry, that we talked about everything but political correctness—well, the reality is that political correctness rests upon some serious political work in this culture in Canada and in America that needs to be done. And what I tried to express was that we didn't have political correctness as long as straight white men were in charge. There was no argument about "Let's get this right." But when people who no longer exercise absolute power still have predominant power, then there's an argument.

And to Michelle's point—about gender, the workplace, race, sexuality and the like—I just think that it was an unnecessarily vigorous, and sometimes sharply worded debate between us all.

RUDYARD GRIFFITHS: Michelle, a final word from you?

MICHELLE GOLDBERG: Well, if you are curious about the Peterson quote that I mentioned about how this experiment with women and men working together is maybe not working, please do google it. It's from an interview with VICE.

Stephen Fry and I could probably have sat on the same side of another debate. But I feel like the phrase "political correctness" has expanded to cover a whole range of challenges. I found it really interesting how much people were talking about their feelings, because when women talk about their feelings, that is "politically correct excess." And when men talk about this feeling that they can't empirically define, we should all change in deference to that.

RUDYARD GRIFFITHS: Okay, guys, great thoughts. Let's go get a drink in the reception.

MICHELLE GOLDBERG: Thank you.

MICHAEL ERIC DYSON: Let's do that, yeah.

ACKNOWLEDGEMENTS

The Munk Debates are the product of the public-spirited-ness of a remarkable group of civic-minded organizations and individuals. First and foremost, these debates would not be possible without the vision and leadership of the Aurea Foundation. Founded in 2006 by Peter and Melanie Munk, the Aurea Foundation supports Canadian individuals and institutions involved in the study and development of public policy. The debates are the foundation's signature initiative, a model for the kind of substantive public policy conversation Canadians can foster globally. Since the creation of the debates in 2008, the foundation has underwritten the entire cost of each semi-annual event. The debates have also benefited from the input and advice of members of the board of the foundation, including Mark Cameron, Andrew Coyne, Devon Cross, Allan Gotlieb, Margaret MacMillan, Anthony Munk, Robert Prichard, and Janice Stein.

For her contribution to the preliminary edit of the book, the debate organizers would like to thank Jane McWhinney.

Since their inception, the Munk Debates have sought to take the discussions that happen at each event to national and international audiences. Here the debates have benefited immeasurably from a partnership with Canada's national newspaper, the *Globe and Mail*, and the counsel of its editor-in-chief, David Walmsley.

With the publication of this superb book, House of Anansi Press is helping the debates reach new audiences in Canada and around the world. The debates' organizers would like to thank Anansi chair Scott Griffin and president and publisher Sarah MacLachlan for their enthusiasm for this book project and insights into how to translate the spoken debate into a powerful written intellectual exchange.

ABOUT THE DEBATERS

MICHAEL ERIC DYSON is an author, professor, and broadcaster. He currently teaches sociology at Georgetown University, hosts the acclaimed "The Michael Eric Dyson Show" on NPR, and is a contributing editor for the *New Republic* and ESPN's website The Undefeated. He has written more than a dozen books on issues of race, culture, and politics in the United States, including the recent *New York Times* bestseller *Tears We Cannot Stop: A Sermon to White America*.

MICHELLE GOLDBERG is a columnist for the *New York Times*, a journalist, and bestselling author. Brooklyn-based Goldberg holds a master of science degree in journalism from the University of California, Berkeley, is a frequent political commentator on MSNBC, and has had her writing featured in the *New Yorker*, *Newsweek*, the *Nation*, the *New Republic*, and the *Guardian*. She is the author of three books, including the award-winning *Kingdom Coming: The Rise of Christian Nationalism.*

STEPHEN FRY is an English actor, screenwriter, author, playwright, journalist, poet, comedian, and film director who studied English literature at the University of Cambridge. He's best known for playing Lord Melchett and other characters in the television comedy series *Blackadder* and the Irish writer Oscar Wilde in the 1997 film *Wilde.* Fry has also written and presented several documentary series, including the Emmy Award–winning *Stephen Fry: The Secret Life of the Manic Depressive.*

JORDAN PETERSON is a professor of psychology at the University of Toronto, a clinical psychologist, and the author of *12 Rules for Life: An Antidote to Chaos.* Peterson received his Ph.D. in clinical psychology from McGill University and has been called "one of the most important thinkers to emerge on the world stage for many years" by the *Spectator.* His online self-help program, The Self Authoring Suite, and his online lectures have been viewed more than forty million times on YouTube.

ABOUT THE EDITOR

RUDYARD GRIFFITHS is the chair of the Munk Debates and a Senior Fellow at the Munk School of Global Affairs and Public Policy. In 2006 he was named one of Canada's "Top 40 under 40" by the *Globe and Mail*. He is the editor of thirteen books on history, politics, and international affairs, including *Who We Are: A Citizen's Manifesto*, which was a *Globe and Mail* Best Book of 2009 and a finalist for the Shaughnessy Cohen Prize for Political Writing. He lives in Toronto with his wife and two children.

ABOUT THE MUNK DEBATES

The Munk Debates are Canada's premier public policy event. Held semi-annually, the debates provide leading thinkers with a global forum to discuss the major public policy issues facing the world and Canada. Each event takes place in Toronto in front of a live audience, and the proceedings are covered by domestic and international media. Participants in recent Munk Debates include Anne Applebaum, Louise Arbour, Robert Bell, Tony Blair, John Bolton, Ian Bremmer, Stephen F. Cohen, Daniel Cohn-Bendit, Paul Collier, Howard Dean, Alain de Botton, Hernando de Soto, Alan Dershowitz, E. J. Dionne, Maureen Dowd, Gareth Evans, Nigel Farage, Mia Farrow, Niall Ferguson, William Frist, Newt Gingrich, Malcolm Gladwell, Jennifer Granholm, David Gratzer, Glenn Greenwald, Stephen Harper, Michael Hayden, Rick Hillier, Christopher Hitchens, Richard Holbrooke, Laura Ingraham, Josef Joffe, Robert Kagan, Garry Kasparov,

Henry Kissinger, Charles Krauthammer, Paul Krugman, Arthur B. Laffer, Lord Nigel Lawson, Stephen Lewis, David Daokui Li, Bjørn Lomborg, Lord Peter Mandelson, Elizabeth May, George Monbiot, Caitlin Moran, Dambisa Moyo, Thomas Mulcair, Vali Nasr, Alexis Ohanian, Camille Paglia, George Papandreou, Steven Pinker, Samantha Power, Vladimir Pozner, Robert Reich, Matt Ridley, David Rosenberg, Hanna Rosin, Simon Schama, Anne-Marie Slaughter, Bret Stephens, Mark Steyn, Kimberley Strassel, Andrew Sullivan, Lawrence Summers, Justin Trudeau, Amos Yadlin, and Fareed Zakaria.

The Munk Debates are a project of the Aurea Foundation, a charitable organization established in 2006 by philanthropists Peter and Melanie Munk to promote public policy research and discussion. For more information, visit www.munkdebates.com.

ABOUT THE INTERVIEWS

Rudyard Griffith's interviews with Michael Eric Dyson, Michelle Goldberg, Stephen Fry, and Jordan Peterson were recorded on May 18, 2018. The Aurea Foundation is gratefully acknowledged for permission to reprint excerpts from the following:

(p. 3) "Michael Eric Dyson in Conversation," by Rudyard Griffiths. Copyright © 2018 Aurea Foundation. Transcribed by Transcript Heroes.

(p. 13) "Michelle Goldberg in Conversation," by Rudyard Griffiths. Copyright © 2018 Aurea Foundation. Transcribed by Transcript Heroes.

(p. 21) "Stephen Fry in Conversation," by Rudyard Griffiths. Copyright © 2018 Aurea Foundation. Transcribed by Transcript Heroes.

Is *American Democracy in Crisis?*
Dionne and Sullivan vs. Gingrich and Strassel

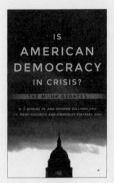

It is the public debate of the moment: Is Donald Trump precipitating a crisis of American democracy? For some the answer is an emphatic "yes." Trump's disregard for the institutions and political norms of U.S. democracy is imperilling the Republic. The sooner his presidency collapses the sooner the healing can begin and the ship of state be righted. For others Trump is not the villain in this drama. Rather, his young presidency is the conduit, not the cause, of America's deep-seated anger toward a privileged and self-dealing Washington elite. Award-winning journalist E. J. Dionne Jr. and influential author and blogger Andrew Sullivan are pitted against former Speaker of the U.S. House of Representatives Newt Gingrich and bestselling author and editor Kimberley Strassel to debate the current crisis of American democracy.

"Our country is now as close to crossing the line from democracy to autocracy as it has been in our lifetimes." —*E. J. Dionne Jr.*

houseofanansi.com/collections/munk-debates

Is This the End of the Liberal International Order?
Niall Ferguson vs. Fareed Zakaria

Since the end of World War II, global affairs have been shaped by the increasing free movement of people and goods, international rules setting, and a broad appreciation of the mutual benefits of a more interdependent world. Together these factors defined the liberal international order and sustained an era of rising global prosperity and declining international conflict. But now, for the first time in a generation, the pillars of liberal internationalism are being shaken to their core by the reassertion of national borders, national interests, and nationalist politics across the globe. Can liberal internationalism survive these challenges and remain the defining rules-based system of the future? Or are we witnessing the beginning of the end of the liberal international order?

"We can no longer confidently talk about a liberal international order. It's become disorder in the sense that democracy has been disrupted." — *Niall Ferguson*

houseofanansi.com/collections/munk-debates

The Global Refugee Crisis: How Should We Respond?
Arbour and Schama vs. Farage and Steyn

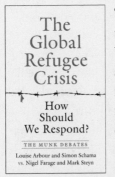

The world is facing the worst humanitarian crisis since the Second World War. Over 300,000 are dead in Syria, and one and a half million are either injured or disabled. Four and a half million people are trying to flee the country. And Syria is just one of a growing number of failed or failing states in the Middle East and North Africa. How should developed nations respond to human suffering on this mass scale? Do the prosperous societies of the West, including Canada and the United States, have a moral imperative to assist as many refugees as they reasonably and responsibly can? Or is this a time for vigilance and restraint in the face of a wave of mass migration that risks upending the tolerance and openness of the West?

"There's nothing to be ashamed of about having an emotional response to the suffering of four million Syrian refugees."
— Simon Schama

Do Humankind's Best Days Lie Ahead?
Pinker and Ridley vs. de Botton and Gladwell

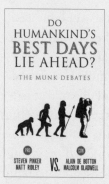

From the Enlightenment onwards, the West has had an enduring belief that through the evolution of institutions, innovations, and ideas, the human condition is improving. But is this the case? Pioneering cognitive scientist Steven Pinker and influential author Matt Ridley take on noted philosopher Alain de Botton and bestselling author Malcolm Gladwell to debate whether humankind's best days lie ahead.

"It's just a brute fact that we don't throw virgins into volcanoes any more. We don't execute people for shoplifting a cabbage. And we used to." —Steven Pinker

Should the West Engage Putin's Russia?
Cohen and Pozner vs. Applebaum and Kasparov

How should the West deal with Vladimir Putin? Acclaimed academic Stephen F. Cohen and veteran journalist and bestselling author Vladimir Pozner square off against internationally renowned expert on Russian history Anne Applebaum and Russian-born political dissident Garry Kasparov to debate the future of the West's relationship with Russia.

"A dictator grows into a monster when he is not confronted at an early stage...And unlike Adolf Hitler, Vladimir Putin has nuclear weapons." —*Garry Kasparov*

Should We Tax the Rich More?
Krugman and Papandreou vs. Gingrich and Laffer

Is imposing higher taxes on the wealthy the best way for countries to reinvest in their social safety nets, education, and infrastructure while protecting the middle class? Or does raising taxes on society's wealth creators lead to capital flight, falling government revenues, and less money for the poor? Nobel Prize–winning economist Paul Krugman and former prime minister of Greece George Papandreou square off against former speaker of the U.S. House of Representatives Newt Gingrich and famed economist Arthur Laffer to debate this key issue.

"The effort to finance Big Government through higher taxes is a direct assault on civil society." —Newt Gingrich

Has the European Experiment Failed?
Joffe and Ferguson vs. Mandelson and Cohn-Bendit

Is one of human history's most ambitious endeavours nearing collapse? Former EU commissioner for trade Peter Mandelson and EU Parliament co-president of the Greens/European Free Alliance Group Daniel Cohn-Bendit debate German publisher-editor and author Josef Joffe and renowned economic historian Niall Ferguson on the future of the European Union.

"For more than ten years, it has been the case that Europe has conducted an experiment in the impossible." —Niall Ferguson

North America's Lost Decade?

Krugman and Rosenberg vs. Summers and Bremmer

The future of the North American economy is more uncertain than ever. In this edition of the Munk Debates, Nobel Prize–winning economist Paul Krugman and chief economist and strategist at Gluskin Sheff + Associates David Rosenberg square off against former U.S. treasury secretary Lawrence Summers and bestselling author Ian Bremmer to tackle the resolution, "Be it resolved: North America faces a Japan-style era of high unemployment and slow growth."

"It's now impossible to deny the obvious, which is that we are not now, and have never been, on the road to recovery." —Paul Krugman

Does the 21st Century Belong to China?
Kissinger and Zakaria vs. Ferguson and Li

Is China's rise unstoppable? Former U.S. secretary of state Henry Kissinger and CNN's Fareed Zakaria pair off against leading historian Niall Ferguson and world-renowned Chinese economist David Daokui Li to debate China's emergence as a global force—the key geopolitical issue of our time.

This edition of the Munk Debates also features the first formal public debate Dr. Kissinger has participated in on China's future.

"I have enormous difficulty imagining a world dominated by China...I believe the concept that any one country will dominate the world is, in itself, a misunderstanding of the world in which we live now." —Henry Kissinger

Hitchens vs. Blair

Christopher Hitchens vs. Tony Blair

Intellectual juggernaut and staunch atheist Christopher Hitchens goes head-to-head with former British prime minister Tony Blair, one of the Western world's most openly devout political leaders, on the age-old question: Is religion a force for good in the world? Few world leaders have had a greater hand in shaping current events than Blair; few writers have been more outspoken and polarizing than Hitchens.

Sharp, provocative, and thoroughly engrossing, *Hitchens vs. Blair* is a rigorous and electrifying intellectual sparring match on the contentious questions that continue to dog the topic of religion in our globalized world.

"If religious instruction were not allowed until the child had attained the age of reason, we would be living in a very different world." —Christopher Hitchens

houseofanansi.com/collections/munk-debates

The Munk Debates: Volume One
Edited by Rudyard Griffiths
Introduction by Peter Munk

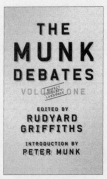

Launched in 2008 by philanthropists Peter and Melanie Munk, the Munk Debates is Canada's premier international debate series, a highly anticipated cultural event that brings together the world's brightest minds.

This volume includes the first five debates in the series and features twenty leading thinkers and doers arguing for or against provocative resolutions that address pressing public policy concerns such as the future of global security, the implications of humanitarian intervention, the effectiveness of foreign aid, the threat of climate change, and the state of health care in Canada and the United States.

"By trying to highlight the most important issues at crucial moments in the global conversation, these debates not only profile the ideas and solutions of some of our brightest thinkers and doers, but crystallize public passion and knowledge, helping to tackle some global challenges confronting humankind."
—*Peter Munk*

houseofanansi.com/collections/munk-debates